The CEO's Guide To Generative Ai
By Kamil Banc

Published by ANC MEDIA LLC
Let's Connect: **kbanc.com**

ISBN: 9798853249165
Copyright © 2023 Kamil Banc All rights reserved.
*Sources and Citations may not always be valid or up to date.

★ ★ ★ ★ ★

If you like this book, consider giving it a review on
Amazon and share it with a friend.

TABLE OF CONTENTS

Why You Should read this book 6
What to expect from this guide 8
Who Wrote This Book? 9

1. Demystifying Generative AI................... 11
What is Generative AI? 11
Automation and Enhanced Decisions 14
Exploring the Capabilities of Gen-AI 15
Future Scope: Beyond Text and Images 17
Limitations, Pros and Cons 19
Integrating AI Capabilities into Your Business 21
Supercharging Your Business.......................... 23

2. Harnessing Gen-AI in Business Operations 25
Streamlining Business Processes...................... 27
Informed Decision-Making 29
Offloading Cognitive Labor to AI...................... 31
Increasing Productivity by Targeting Menial Tasks ... 32
Directly Adding Value to Business Outputs 33
Measuring Success...................................... 35
Crisis Management and Preventing Bottlenecks 37
Seamless Integration into Existing Workflows 38
Engaging Stakeholders 39
Maximizing ROI by Implementing Gen-AI............ 41

3. Cognitive Offloading and Gen-AI 44
Preserving Human Cognition 45
Enhancing Productivity and Satisfaction 46
Why Outperforming Humans Is a good Thing........ 48
A Cognitive Force Multiplier 49

4. Gen-AI and Effective Leadership 52
Building Stronger Relationships with AI Tools 53
Self-Reflection and Leadership........................ 55
Maintaining Trust, Dignity, and Respect 57
Prioritizing Privacy and Ethical Use of Data 58
Self-Improvement for Leaders 59

5. Navigating the Impact of Gen-AI................ 63
Quantifying AI's Cost Savings......................... 64
Unlocking Value 65
Creativity and Art in the AI Domain................... 67
Strategic Analysis and Reasoning 69
Harmonizing AI and Human Development 70
Addressing Job Loss and Other Challenges 71
Navigating New Capabilities, Opportunities, and Threats 72

Closing Thoughts.................................... 75

Appendix... 77
Exercise Guide.. 78
FAQ 89
Glossary.. 97

WHY YOU SHOULD READ THIS BOOK

"The CEO's Guide to Generative AI" is your entry point into understanding the transformative potential of generative AI in business, focusing not on fleeting trends but foundational knowledge. This introductory guide is layered with comprehensive overviews, real-world applications, and strategic insights, all designed to accelerate your familiarity with generative AI and its implications.

Technological evolution waits for no one, it's relentless, rapid, and revolutionary. Keeping pace isn't about a fleeting infatuation with the latest platform or the trendiest solution; instead, it's about cultivating a deep-seated curiosity. A curiosity that drives continuous learning, encourages adaptability, and fuels informed decision-making.

This book isn't tied to a singular technology or tool but offers a broader perspective, exploring the varied facets of generative AI and how they can be leveraged to drive business growth. It aims to pique your curiosity, drawing you into the enthralling world of AI, while providing the knowledge needed to make informed decisions. It equips you to either directly engage with the complex world of AI or hire a professional armed with the necessary knowledge, with the end goal of positioning your organization for long-term success.

One of my goals when writing this book was to have a practical guide that delivers value to the reader no matter what page they open. That's why you don't have to worry about reading all of it in one session. Rather, treat it like a curiosity companion. You see something in the TOC that you are curious about? Go straight to that page, I have made sure to mention many aspects of the topic multiple times so that its easily digestible no matter where in the book you end up.

Embrace "The CEO's Guide to Generative AI" as a launching pad for your journey into the world of artificial intelligence. This is the first step of many into a future where technology and business strategy intertwine, where you can steer your organization nimbly through every wave of technological innovation that looms on the horizon. Your journey starts here.

WHAT TO EXPECT FROM THIS GUIDE

This book aims to illuminate, not overwhelm. It explores the possibilities of generative AI so leaders can ask the right strategic questions. Implementation details will evolve rapidly - the key is starting with the right foundation.

Don't expect step-by-step instructions. Do anticipate thought-provoking perspectives to integrate AI into business objectives. The focus is guiding you to opportunities, not tactics.

Wondering where to find an AI expert? That's the next step after reading. This book sparks the vision - a growing field of specialists can help realize it.

AI talent doesn't fit neatly into IT. It requires new roles like Chief AI Officer. But again, first comes establishing priorities and strategy.

Let this book be your flashlight into the complex AI landscape. It shines a light on key areas so you can navigate confidently. With the right questions framed, you can find solutions that fit your unique organization.

The core purpose is setting you up to succeed with AI amidst uncertainty. By understanding the potential, you can lead effectively into this rapidly changing frontier.

Let me know if you would like me to modify or expand on this draft summary further. I aimed to set appropriate expectations and explain the strategic focus of the book based on the feedback provided.

WHO WROTE THIS BOOK?

Hi, I'm Kamil Banc. A passionate AI optimist and business consultant for some of the world's biggest companies, helping them use advanced systems to improve how they work and be more productive. As the Chief AI Officer (CAIO) at Kwik Brain, I am deeply involved in practical uses of these systems in business, an area I've focused more and more on in my career.

Born in Soviet-occupied Eastern Europe, I got smuggled into Western Germany at the tender age of 18 months, where I grew up. In 2009, I made the leap to America, a journey that has been key to my personal and professional progress.

In recent years, I've specialized in the rapidly changing technology industry, starting Adapt & Create (adaptandcreate.com), a consulting firm. Through Adapt & Create, we're dedicated to improving business operations through the implementation of AI, offering specialized services like the Ignition Kit, designed to strategically apply these systems to improve business performance.

I've also developed and worked on AI-assisted projects, like publishing children's books, launching a creative fairytale- news-network, hosting master-mind-groups, fundraising, and other activities to demonstrate the potential of this transformative technology. I strongly believe in the power of storytelling in today's world and see activities like this as a way to get more people interested in these fascinating developments.

Throughout my journey, I've seen first-hand how businesses can benefit from using the power of nimble technology adaptation. I've been approached by business leaders from around the world, eager to understand and use its potential of artificial intelligence. This sparked the idea to write "The CEO's Guide to Generative AI". The book breaks down this complex new f rontier, turning it into understandable, actionable information that can help business leaders use its transformative power.

On social media platforms like YouTube, Twitter (@kamilbanc), and LinkedIn, I often talk about this topic so feel free to connect with me there.

My journey has taken me from my roots in Eastern Europe to leading technology initiatives across America and the globe today. It's been an adventure full of twists and turns, but along the way I've learned to focus on what I can control - continuously learning, adapting and creating in this rapidly changing world.

The goal of this book is to see these emerging technologies as tools to boost human abilities, not replace them. By keeping an open mindset and using innovations like these responsibly and ethically, we can use them to increase human intelligence and empower people. I invite you to join me and find out how.

1

DEMYSTIFYING
GENERATIVE AI

Begin your transformational by understanding the fundamental aspects of *Generative AI (moving forward Gen- AI)*. In clear, concise, and engaging language, this chapter breaks down AI's complex universe into digestible pieces. I'll help business leaders unearth the powerful impact it can have on automation and decision-shaping processes in your organization. You'll delve into the wide-ranging capabilities of Gen-AI and imagine its future scope - hint: it's not all about text and images. The chapter will guide you on integrating these AI capabilities into your very own business landscape to gain a competitive edge.

I want you to harness technology to supercharge your business; this includes how you can take advantage of AI in making informed decisions, enhancing efficiencies, and achieving remarkable growth. From understanding what Gen- AI is to exploring how it can revolutionize your organization's processes, this chapter is your first step towards becoming a true AI advocate, pioneer, and leader. As a result, you'll be fully equipped with knowledge and practical implications of Gen-AI, all tailored to your organizational sphere and needs. Discover how you can move towards the future, today.

WHAT IS GENERATIVE AI?

Gen-AI represents a cutting-edge application in the broader realm of artificial intelligence. As a CEO, you may have heard this term bandied around in tech-savvy circles or in forward-thinking board meetings, but what does it really mean for you and your organization?

Gen-AI represents a cutting-edge application in the broader realm of artificial intelligence. You may have heard this term thrown around in tech-savvy circles or in forward- thinking board meetings, but what does it really mean for you and your organization?

At its core, Gen-AI refers to systems capable of creating something new from pre-existing data. Unlike traditional models that merely interpret input data and make predictions, these generative models have the remarkable ability to generate new, unseen data that mirrors the original dataset.

Now, you may be wondering, why is this particularly important for businesses? Well, the possibilities are endless.

Suppose you're in a product-based company. Gen-AI can be used to design new products based on trends gleaned from historical data. Not only can this shave off precious time and resources from your R&D department, it can deliver innovative products tailored to your customer's needs like never before.

Think about customer service. Imagine a model trained on your past interactions with customers. Gen-AI, using this amassed data, can create in-depth responses to customer inquiries, helping them feel understood and valued.

Importantly, Gen-AI doesn't just replicate, it learns, adjusts, and creates based on patterns it's picked up during the training process. This makes it a powerful tool for businesses wishing to streamline operations, explore new avenues of innovation, and elevate their value propositions.

To put it simply, Gen-AI is AI's imaginative cousin. It's not just about understanding the world; it's about building a new one based on the knowledge it seamlessly assimilates. As the leader of your organization, harnessing the power of Gen-AI could revolutionize the way you conduct business, propelling you miles ahead in your industry's competitive landscape.

Where Does Generative AI Fit In?

Artificial Intelligence, or AI, equips computers with the capability to mirror human-like decision-making processes. It's the technology that gives machines a semblance of human intellect.

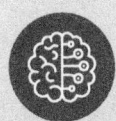

A subset of AI is **Machine Learning,** a process through which computers can enhance their performance over time by identifying patterns and learning from data, much like humans learn from experience.

Deep Learning takes machine learning a notch further. It's akin to cultivating an innate sense of understanding in machines, enabling them to recognize complex patterns in data, similar to a seasoned detective who can deduce a situation from the smallest of clues.

Generative AI represents the apex of this technological evolution. It leverages pre-existing knowledge, gleaned from extensive data, to generate new content. Imagine an accomplished novelist using their vast reading experience to craft unique, captivating stories. This is what generative AI can accomplish in its domain.

AUTOMATION AND ENHANCED DECISIONS

As you operate in your leadership role, the question, "How do I optimize my organization's performance and decision- making capabilities?" becomes more pertinent. That's where the power of automation and decision enhancement come into play, augmented greatly by Gen-AI.

Automation is more than a buzzword in today's business landscape. It's about leveraging technology, specifically Gen- AI, to streamline manual, error-prone tasks and bring agility to your operations. Whether it's in document handling, email responses, data entry, or even customer service, automating these backend processes accelerates business operations and minimizes potential for human error.

What does this mean for you as a leader? More efficient business operations lead to faster turnaround times, increased productivity, and ultimately, improved profit margins. But there's more to it. Automation also offers cognitive relief to your teams by handling high-volume, repetitive tasks, freeing them to focus on complex, creative, and strategic aspects of your business.

Now, let's talk about decision enhancement. In the realm of business, every decision significance. But, making these critical choices is often fraught with uncertainties. Gen-AI provides a pathway to informed, data-driven decision making, thereby reducing the risk associated with gut-based decisions.

Gen-AI takes the data your organization generates or collects, learns from it, recognizes patterns, and ultimately predicts future outcomes. Say goodbye to hit-and-miss strategies. With AI-driven insights, your strategies can be laser-focused and results-driven.

Let's consider an example in the realm of marketing. Gen- AI can help craft customer-centric marketing strategies by analyzing and predicting consumer behavior patterns from your data. You could effectively predict your customer's preferences and tailor your marketing campaigns accordingly, maximizing their impact.

In essence, as a business leader, leveraging this technology can give you the twofold advantage of automation and decision enhancement. Embrace the power of this technology to not only outdo your competitors but redefine leadership in the AI era.

EXPLORING THE CAPABILITIES OF GEN-AI

You're now aware of what Gen-AI is and its profound impact on automation and decision enhancement. But how far can we take this technology? Let's delve into some exciting capabilities of Gen-AI that can have tangible benefits for your organization.

1. **Content Generation:** One of the most obvious uses of Gen-AI is in content creation, be it text, images, or even virtual reality environments. From drafting engaging blog posts and newsletters to creating personalized marketing messages, Gen-AI can streamline and enhance the creative process.

2. **Product Design:** These systems can help design new products or optimize existing designs based on specific parameters and constraints. From optimizing packaging for space and cost to creating appealing aesthetics for targeted demographics, it can transform your product development process.

3. **Predictive Analytics:** Equipped with sophisticated tools, you can analyze patterns within large data sets and make predictions about future trends and behaviors. This can drastically improve the decision-making process across multiple functions, like sales, supply chain, and finance.

4. **Personalization:** Given the ubiquity of data, personalization is more achievable and crucial than ever. Gen-AI can analyze individual patterns and preferences to deliver highly customized experiences, be it in product recommendations, customer service, or user experiences.

5. **Risk Mitigation:** Gen-AI can be thoroughly trained on different scenarios to predict potential risks and suggest countermeasures. It could help in detecting potential fraud, mitigating cybersecurity threats, or foreseeing market volatility.

Looking forward, these are just the beginnings of the truly transformational possibilities Gen-AI can bring to table. Adopting and harnessing its power will not only make your organization more efficient and profitable, but also more innovative and future-ready. As a forward-looking leader, recognize the capabilities of Gen-AI and seize the opportunities it presents.

> *72% of business leaders believe AI will have a significant impact on their organization within 2 years*

Source: *https://www.pwc.com/gx/en/issues/data-and-analytics/publications/artificial-intelligence- study.html*

FUTURE SCOPE: BEYOND TEXT AND IMAGES

Gen-AI has already made impressive strides in content creation, spanning text, image, and even audio outputs. But the horizon of AI expands far beyond these domains. Let's venture into the future, a realm brimming with possibilities and potentialities waiting to be harnessed.

1. **Augmented Reality (AR) and Virtual Reality (VR):** Create immersive AR and VR environments that respond dynamically to user behavior or external data. Imagine virtual training programs that adapt to a user's learning style or progress, making learning more engaging and effective.

2. **Custom Manufacturing:** Customization could become the new norm. Imagine AI systems designing and manufacturing products tailored to individual customer's needs and preferences. This could revolutionize industries from fashion to automobiles.

3. **Healthcare Diagnosis and Treatment:** We could use those tools to aid in the diagnosis and treatment of diseases, by generating simulations based on patient data. It could predict the progression of diseases and the effect of different treatment regimens, empowering doctors to make informed decisions for personalized patient treatment.

4. **Climate Modeling and Disaster Prevention:** Advanced models could predict future climate patterns, helping us better prepare for or even prevent natural disasters. By correlating vast amounts of data across time and space, this technology could help us in organizing mitigative measures.

5. **Entertainment and Gaming:** From creating diversified characters and narratives to developing implementing adaptive gameplay that responds to a player's actions, Gen- AI is set to redefine the future of entertainment and gaming.

THE CEO'S GUIDE TO **GENERATIVE AI**

While the advancements may sound fantastical, they are not mere pipe dreams. We currently stand at the precipice of an AI revolution that promises to transform our world in unprecedented ways. As a forward-thinking leader, acknowledging the future scope and possibilities can help in identifying new avenues of growth and pioneering innovative solutions that will leave a lasting imprint in your industry.

> *40% of organizations increased their AI budgets in 2022 compared to 2021*

Source: *https://www2.deloitte.com/xe/en/insights/industry/tec technology-media-and-telecom- predictions/2022/ai-investment-business-impact.html*

LIMITATIONS, PROS AND CONS

Embracing AI systems in your business holds vast untapped potential for enhancing operations and decision- making processes. However, with such advancements come inevitable obstacles that businesses will need to counter. The crucial decision point remains whether these challenges can be mitigated by the potential value offered by such an innovative approach.

A significant hurdle is harmonizing these advanced models with established legacy systems. This can be resource-heavy and complex. For example, a financial institution unwilling to abandon time-tested protocol might encounter obstacles when trying to coalesce this cutting- edge output with its existing systems.

Furthermore, regulating and safeguarding the quality of content crafted by such automated solutions can prove challenging. The awe-inspiring speed at which content can be generated often necessitates critical human interaction to ensure its accuracy, relevance, and overall quality. Should an entity like a marketing firm use this solution for content creation, it might produce an impressive quantity of content, yet each output could still require human revision to assure alignment with a defined tone, quality criteria, and relevancy. Therefore, the necessity for continuous oversight persists.

The element of emotional understanding also plays a pivotal role. Lack of emotional intelligence can result in content that may lack intuitive, creative, or personal human touch. This becomes crucial in industries where empathy and human interaction strongly affect outcomes, such as customer service or hospitality.

Data availability and quality are fundamental to the success of the model. It needs a rich repository of high- quality data for optimum function. Thus, businesses with limited data resources may not be in a position to extract full value from these systems.

The complex nature of these models implies a significant investment in key areas, including specialized equipment, and knowledgeable personnel for operation and maintenance.

Determining the applicability of automated models requires a careful evaluation of challenges and benefits. Given the positive implications, most businesses can identify areas where automation can offer tangible benefits, such as enhancing productivity, automating repetitive tasks, or boosting creativity. The subsequent step involves reviewing the feasibility of the model's implementation within existing structures, necessitating a deep understanding of technical and operational facets and resource allocation.

Adhering to ethical standards is critical and directly impacts brand reputation and customer trust. It is paramount that the usage of such technologies aligns with organizational values and stakeholder interests.

The level of human oversight required cannot be underestimated. Certain industries may call for stricter controls than others, depending upon the nature of the enterprise.

Lastly, gauging the return-on-investment can help balance resource allocation and potential rewards. Rather than adopting technology just for the sake of being technologically advanced, it's about fully maximizing its potential while effectively managing risks. A measured approach enables businesses to decisively strategize their transition to automation integration, fully reaping the associated benefits.

INTEGRATING AI CAPABILITIES INTO YOUR BUSINESS

Integrating Gen-AI into your business is no trivial task. It's a step-by-step process that requires careful planning, execution, and maintenance. However, the rewards of successfully integrating AI can be transformative, unlocking new levels of efficiency, productivity, and innovation.

Firstly, identifying the areas of your business that can significantly benefit from AI is crucial. It could be a department that handles vast amounts of data, a function struggling with menial and repetitive tasks, or a process that needs predictive insights for decision-making. Understanding the context and needs of these areas will guide you in the adoption of the right AI tool.

Once the areas have been defined, it's time to align the adoption with your overall business strategy. The goal of AI integration should not merely be about technology deployment, but how it advances your business goals. From enhancing customer satisfaction to driving operational efficiency or even fostering innovation, the AI tool you choose should be geared to propel your strategic objectives forward.

The next stage involves sourcing the right AI tools and ensuring they are appropriately tweaked to your business requirements. This is where you might need to partner with AI solution providers, who can help translate your business needs into functional AI algorithms. Building a mutual understanding with such partners can speed up the design and implementation phase.

A critical aspect that often gets overlooked in the integration phase is staff training. Your employees must be prepared and equipped to work alongside AI tools for best results. Training sessions can cover various aspects, from fundamental knowledge of AI to hands-on experience operating the new tools. Remember, AI is there to augment human capabilities, not replace them. Thus fostering a culture of collaboration between your staff and AI is key.

In the final phase, constant monitoring and tweaking are essential. Like any business process, AI integration should be continually assessed and updated for optimal performance. Regular feedback from staff who interact with these tools can provide invaluable insights for fine-tuning them.

While this transition may seem daunting, the infusion of AI into your business could be the game changer that skyrockets your company's growth. With a steady approach, grounded in understanding and strategic alignment, integrating AI capabilities into your business can become a smooth and rewarding journey.

> *JP Morgan uses generative AI to write research reports and equity notes. This greatly increases analyst productivity*

Source: *https://www.businessinsider.com/jpmorgan-using-ai-to-write-research-reports-and-trade-ideas-2020-2*

SUPERCHARGING YOUR BUSINESS

The key to energizing your business lies in leveraging transformative new technologies. This means utilizing advanced systems to enhance operations, deliver stellar customer service, and uncover fresh opportunities.

Consider Gen-AI as rocket fuel for your processes - an energy source propelling increased efficiency and reduced errors. Whether it's data analysis, project management or customer interactions, these systems can optimize and automate tasks. This enables your team to focus on strategic business aspects. By relieving repetitive task burden, you can accomplish more with less - reduced time, effort and cost.

Moreover, these technologies revolutionize customer service. By understanding, learning from and predicting customer behavior, you can offer hyper-personalized service to each customer. It's about comprehending needs even before expressed - a foresight elevating satisfaction, loyalty and reputation.

The potential doesn't stop there. These systems also enable uncovering and seizing new opportunities, paving the way for innovation and expansion. By simulating scenarios, analyzing trends and predicting outcomes, informed decisions become possible around new products, markets or business models. It's like having a crystal ball navigating the future confidently.

However, as with any powerful tool, responsible and ethical use is essential, including ensuring transparency and respecting privacy.

In summary, energizing your business with these technologies means amplifying capabilities, outperforming competition, and steering towards a future where innovation and growth are the norm. This technology leap could be the catalyst propelling your business to new heights.

THE CEO'S GUIDE TO **GENERATIVE AI**

DEMYSTIFYING
GENERATIVE AI

Exercise 1:

Identify areas of your business that would benefit from automation or enhanced decision-making capabilities. Create a wish list of areas where you'd like to see improvements and explore how AI can address these needs.

Exercise 2:

Engage your team in a brainstorming session to imagine what future AI innovations could look like in your organization. Foster an open dialogue about fears, hopes, and expectations for AI.

*Detailed exercise guides can be found in the appendix

2
HARNESSING GEN-AI IN BUSINESS OPERATIONS

In this chapter we delve into the practical aspects of implementing Gen-AI into your daily operations. As a CEO, decision-maker, or leader, you'll explore ways to streamline your business processes, making tedious tasks efficient and effective with its help. You'll find actionable strategies to augment your decision-making capabilities. Learn how to delegate menial tasks to AI, thus enabling cognitive offloading and better focusing your team's mental bandwidth on strategic tasks that require human touch and finesse.

This chapter also elaborates on how Gen-AI can add direct value to your business outputs, fundamentally changing the way you view productivity and measure success within your organization. In a rapidly evolving business landscape, crisis management and preventing bottlenecks become paramount. As such, you'll understand ways to leverage AI in these areas for optimum results.

Furthermore, embracing new technology isn't about creating disruptions. Instead, it's about seamlessly integrating its functions into your current workflows, causing as little friction as possible. This chapter teaches you how to achieve that integration in the most effective manner.

Finally, you will gain insights into how to keep all stakeholders engaged and informed about your AI operations, enhancing their trust and participation. The knowledge gained from this chapter will equip you to revolutionize your business operations, increase productivity, and maximize efficiency.

THE CEO'S GUIDE TO **GENERATIVE AI**

> *Netflix employs generative AI to generate personalized movie and show recommendations for each subscriber. This has improved customer retention*

Source: *https://netflixtechblog.com/algorithms-for-recommender-systems-bd9c8a8e615c*

STREAMLINING BUSINESS PROCESSES

One of the most transformative impacts of AI lies in its ability to streamline business processes. Conventionally, the broad range of operations in a business, from data entry to resource management, involve a significant amount of manual oversight. These processes, despite their critical importance, often consume substantial time and resources, potentially slowing down growth and innovation.

These tools are especially helpful when it comes to automating these tasks, thereby driving efficiency and saving time. For instance, think of invoice processing - a task that is repetitive and time-consuming. With the right algorithm, companies can automate this task, and instead, focus human resources on processes that require more strategic intervention.

Moreover, Gen-AI can recognize complex patterns in data faster than any human team. It can make accurate predictions, helping organizations take proactive actions rather than awaiting crises and resolving them retrospectively. This improved efficiency is not restricted to one business area; it can be replicated across departments - from HR to operations to finance.

Consistency is another benefit provided by these tools. Traditional business operations can be prone to human error. Even the smallest miscalculations or oversight can lead to financial loss or can damage a business's reputation. By utilizing AI, we can avoid these missteps, improve accuracy, and ensure there's a consistent standard of operations across the organization.

Integrating AI into business operations is not about replacing human labor but enhancing it. When properly deployed, it can help organizations become leaner, faster, and more productive. It can free up cognitive and physical resources, allowing humans to do what we are truly best at: innovating, strategizing, and nurturing relationships.

THE CEO'S GUIDE TO **GENERATIVE AI**

Remember, tech-integration is a journey, not a switch to be flipped overnight. It requires a strategy, investment, and ongoing oversight. However, with proper planning and utilization, the benefits can be transformative and long- lasting.

> *AI augmentation is expected to double the productivity of an average worker by 2035*

Source: *https://www.mckinsey.com/featured-insights/artificial-intelligence/ai-productivity-and-the-future- of-work-an-economist-perspective*

INFORMED DECISION-MAKING

Traditionally, business decisions are based on historical data, subjective judgment, and often gut instinct. Although this model has its strengths, it can sometimes lead to misjudgments, particularly when enormous amounts of data are involved or when the turnaround time is crucial. Gen-AI can transform this landscape, making decision-making more informed and precise.

First, let's understand how it can facilitate strong data interpretation, a key aspect of informed decision-making. These models can analyze vast amounts of data, find correlations and patterns, and present insights that may not be readily visible to the human eye. They can process and make sense of big data faster than any conventional data analytics method, making it a powerful tool for decision- makers who rely on complex data to strategize and move business forward.

Moreover, your artificial decision-assistant is predictive. It's not just about understanding where you are now, it's about predicting where you can go. By analyzing past and present data patterns, it can anticipate outcomes, trends, and scenarios. This predictive capability empowers decision- makers with insights about what could come next, enabling them to strategize and take action proactively.

Depending on the initial training data, this technology also has the potential to removing decision-making bias. Human decisions can be influenced by a variety of cognitive biases that can disrupt objective judgment. Gen-AI, however, operates by analyzing data using predefined algorithms, devoid of emotions, therefore providing a bias-free perspective.

Finally, Gen-AI fosters adaptability. In a rapidly changing economic and tech environment, decisions need to be constantly reevaluated and updated. These systems can learn and adapt from new data, ensuring decision-making remains relevant and timely.

Achieving the right balance between human intelligence and artificial intelligence in decision-making is crucial. The human touch, empathy, ethical consideration, and big picture thinking coupled with the analytical power, accuracy, speed, and adaptability of AI, can create a potent combination for effective and informed decision-making.

> *By 2030, AI could deliver up to $15.7 trillion to the global economy, contributing an additional 1.2% GDP growth per year*

Source: *https://www.pwc.com/gx/en/issues/data-and-analytics/publications/artificial-intelligence- study.html*

OFFLOADING COGNITIVE LABOR TO AI

In my opinion, cognitive capacity will be a determining business resource going forward. Offloading cognitive labor, thus freeing human minds to focus on more valuable and strategic tasks will become one of the biggest advantages in business. Cognitive labor encapsulates mental tasks and efforts that often consume a notable amount of time and energy. These can range from data analysis to scheduling tasks. While these tasks are essential, they can take away time and mental resources from activities that are exclusive to human capabilities such as critical thinking, creativity, and emotional intelligence. That's where offloading cognitive labor to automated systems can profoundly transform the efficiency and productivity of an organization.

By automating repetitive tasks, you can cut down cognitive burden. Gen-AI efficiently performs functions such as data mining, bookkeeping, scheduling, projection making, and many more under a set of defined rules and patterns, all while minimizing human error.

Beyond automation, you can use these tools analyze, learn, and make decisions based on enormous data sets, tasks that would overwhelm the human brain. By taking over such activities, AI allows humans to focus less on data crunching and more on strategic tasks like interpreting the outcomes, strategizing or forming creative solutions.

Alongside these practical benefits, offloading cognitive labor also positively impacts employee well-being. Mental overload can lead to increased stress and decreased productivity. By reducing these factors, your employees can maintain better focus and prevent burnout, leading to improved job satisfaction and productivity.

However, it's essential to note the importance of ethical considerations when it comes to respecting privacy regulations and ensuring that data is handled responsibly. These technical and ethical challenges can be successfully navigated with the right training, guidelines, and foresight.

Ultimately, the goal is not to replace human cognitive labor with AI but to create a symbiotic relationship where routine tasks are managed automatically, and more complex, creative and ethical decisions remain within the human domain. This enhanced collaboration paves the way for a more productive, efficient, and innovative workplace.

INCREASING PRODUCTIVITY BY TARGETING MENIAL TASKS

Productivity and efficiency have always been vital to effective business operations. However, menial and mundane tasks often take up a substantial portion of an employee's time, demanding cognitive resources that could be better utilized for critical thinking or creative solutions. Gen-AI offers a compelling solution to this issue by taking over these routine tasks, increasing overall productivity.

For instance, consider data entry, a process common in many organizations. This task, while essential for maintaining records, is time-consuming and leaves room for error, affecting overall operational efficiency. Simple errors in entering data can lead to complications down the line which can take significant time and resources to rectify. Gen-AI, being capable of processing large amounts of data quickly and with a high degree of accuracy, can automate this task, eliminating human errors and freeing up valuable time for employees to focus on more strategic tasks.

But remember, automation is only the first step. Gen-AI also has the capacity to learn from its actions and improve over time, which is invaluable for tasks such as client communication or customer service. With the ability to learn from previous interactions and adapt its responses, AI can manage routine customer queries efficiently, providing rapid resolutions and enhancing overall customer service while enabling human customer service representatives to handle more complex issues.

Transferring tasks to AI requires thoughtful and strategic implementation. It's vital to maintain a balance between the efficiencies provided by automation and the innate abilities humans bring to work, such as creative problem-solving and emotional intelligence.

Reskilling or upskilling your employees to manage, interpret, and deploy AI systems effectively will be essential going forward, but even here, AI can be of service and help you design custom training and implementation workshops. It's not about replacing humans with machines, but rather, enabling humans to leverage machines for increased efficiency and productivity.

If appropriately deployed, organizations will be enabled to create a more streamlined, efficient, and productive environment. By targeting menial tasks, AI empowers the workforce to focus on strategic, creative, and engaging tasks, leading to a more satisfying and productive work experience.

DIRECTLY ADDING VALUE TO BUSINESS OUTPUTS

There is tremendous potential in directly adding value to business outputs that goes beyond automating tasks to improve efficiency. AI technologies can generate insights and solutions that can transform the way your business operates and interacts with customers.

Take, for instance, the use of Gen-AI in product development. From helping you analyze vast amounts of customer feedback data, to determine patterns, and generating insights about what your customers want. Applying this knowledge can assist in creating products that more closely align with customer needs and wants, increasing the value of your product output.

Or how about revolutionizing your marketing efforts? For instance, Gen-AI can create personalized customer interactions based on customers' past interactions, preferences, and behavior. These personalized interactions can drastically enhance customer engagement and satisfaction, consequently boosting customer loyalty and fostering long-term relationships.

In the realm of finance and forecasting, AI can sift through past financial data, understand market trends, and make future projections. Such data-driven insights and predictions bring a higher level of accuracy to financial decisions leading to improved profitability.

Another example could be the management and optimization of supply chains. By processing mountains of data far quicker than humans, AI can predict potential disruptions, or identify inefficiencies, helping organizations enact proactive measures to mitigate risks or issues before they become significant problems.

In all of these cases, the key is that Gen-AI not only aids in the execution of operations but can also provide strategic insights and predictions derived from vast amounts of data. This creates a significant opportunity for businesses to enhance their outputs, improve their decision-making, and create tangible value.

Please keep in mind that just like other advancements over the last couple of decades, Gen-AI is not a magic bullet. It's a tool, and like all tools, its effectiveness depends significantly on how it's utilized. However, with a strategic approach and mindful implementation, the potential for directly adding value to business outputs is enormous.

MEASURING SUCCESS

Measuring success with AI is integral to understanding the impact and effectiveness of the technology within your organization. Unlike traditional performance metrics that focus on results alone, quantifying AI success requires a holistic view, mapping both output and the processes leading up to it.

One of the foremost ways to measure the success of AI is by evaluating the improvement in efficiency and productivity. For example, if an AI system is implemented for customer service, its success can be gauged by monitoring the reduction in response times or increase in customer satisfaction scores. Similarly, in a manufacturing setting, the decrease in production time or the improvement in product quality after integrating an AI system would determine its effectiveness.

Another solid indicator of AI success is the degree of reduction in human errors. For instance, if Gen-AI is employed for financial record keeping or data entry tasks, a marked decrease in discrepancies or mistakes would indicate successful AI implementation.

Moreover, the ability to offload cognitive labor and free up employees for more strategic tasks is another measure of AI success. By tracking how much time your employees used to spend on menial tasks and how much more strategic work they are now able to take on, you can quantify the benefits of AI integration.

Savings in cost and resources are another hallmark of successful AI implementation. Using AI for activities like energy management or inventory control can lead to significant reductions in operational costs, providing tangible proof of AI success.

It's also important to measure the effectiveness of AI from an innovation perspective. AI's capability to analyze and learn from vast amounts of data can lead to breakthrough insights and novel solutions. The success of these innovations, whether it's a new product developed or a transformed business process, is a testament to the efficacy of the AI tools in place.

Finally, customer satisfaction and engagement should also be considered when measuring AI success. With AI's ability for personalization, organizations can offer tailored experiences to their customers. Improvements in customer engagement metrics, customer retention, and even growth in the customer base can be directly linked back to successful AI implementation.

Remember, measuring success with AI is not a one-time step, but a continuous process. Regular monitoring and evaluation should be an integral part of your organization's AI strategy to ensure it continually adds value and adapts to changing needs and circumstances.

One of the most amazing aspects of Large Language Models (LLMs) is that they are very well adept to interpret and understand qualitative data. Instead of only counting how many 5 star reviews you got on your testimonial page, these models can also interpret customer sentiment based on their actual written review and draw conclusions from that.

CRISIS MANAGEMENT AND PREVENTING BOTTLENECKS

In the fast-paced and dynamic world of business, crises and bottlenecks are inevitable. Organizations who use these new platforms and tools are now better equipped to manage these unexpected hurdles while preventing potential bottlenecks.

Crisis management often involves quickly processing vast amounts of data to understand the situation and make informed decisions. Gen-AI excels at this. When a crisis strikes, AI can analyze historical data, current market trends, customer behavior, and other relevant factors swiftly, providing a comprehensive understanding of the situation. This rapid analysis allows organizations to act quickly and effectively, limiting the potential damage.

For instance, let's consider the challenges posed by sudden market changes or regulatory updates. AI tools can quickly scan industry-wide data, recognize the changes, calculate their potential impact, and propose strategic responses. These insights equip organizations to respond proactively to crises and even convert them into opportunities.

When it comes to preventing bottlenecks, AI greatly helps in optimizing business workflows. AI can predict potential bottlenecks by analyzing patterns in data and recognizing where delays or blockages might occur. For instance, in a supply chain, AI algorithms can monitor logistic data and predict potential disruptions based on external factors such as weather conditions or sudden demand fluctuations.

More integrated and advanced systems can help reroute resources when spotting a potential bottlenecks, ensuring operations flow seamlessly. For example, in a warehouse operation, if an AI-enabled system predicts a bottleneck in the packaging area due to an influx of orders, it could reallocate personnel from less busy areas to handle this increase in demand.

With every challenge faced, these systems continually learn and improve, effectively reshaping their strategies to better manage future disruptions.

Organizations equipped with such tools will thrive when it comes to managing crises effectively and preventing operational bottlenecks, enhancing business agility, resilience, and long-term success. It's about moving from being reactive to being proactive, providing a powerful competitive edge in today's complex business environment.

SEAMLESS INTEGRATION INTO EXISTING WORKFLOWS

The integration of Gen-AI into existing workflows is an essential step. And contrary to common perception, this needn't be an invasive process. AI can be implemented in a way that arouses minimal disruption to existing operations, making its adoption smoother and more efficient.

A key aspect of the seamless integration is to start by identifying tasks in your current workflow that can be easily automated or improved. Simple and repetitive tasks such as data entry or scheduling are suitable initial targets as AI can greatly simplify these tasks with minimal changes to the existing process.

Integrating AI often becomes an evolution in the tools your employees are already using and can be as easy as upgrading the tools to the lates version and then training your employees how to use the new features. Often, tech can be added onto existing software or platforms to enhance their utility. For instance, an AI-powered chatbot can be integrated with your current customer service platform to automatically handle low complexity queries, allowing your customer service team to focus on more complex issues.

A big step when it comes to seamless integration also hinges on preparing the workforce for the changes in their work environment moving forward. This involves proper training and support to help employees understand the benefits of their new tools and how to use them effectively. When employees see these instruments as an opportunity to augment their performance rather than a threat to their jobs, they are more likely to embrace it. The key here is to ensure AI integration amplifies human potential and doesn't overshadow it.

Another pillar of successful integration should have iterative feedback channels. This helps in adjusting the system according to practical requirements and can drastically improve the fit within existing workflows.

A case in point can be the retail sector. Adopting AI in inventory forecasting can be smoothly integrated into existing workflows. As the resulting forecasts are more precise based on the analysis of vast data and evolving trends, this can eliminate overstocking and understocking issues and enhance supply chain efficiency without major disruptions to existing operations.

Lastly, it's important to remember, AI integration is not a goal - it's a journey of constant learning and evolution, adapting and improving as you better understand the capability of AI and the unique needs of your workflow. With the right approach, AI can become an indispensable part of your operations, working alongside your staff to achieve greater efficiency and productivity.

ENGAGING STAKEHOLDERS

Stakeholders, both internal and external, play significant roles in shaping and deploying AI strategies and tools. Engaging them early on is an integral part of a smooth adoption.

Beginning with **internal stakeholders,** these individuals are directly involved in the day-to-day operations of your organization. Employees, department heads, managers, and executives stand to benefit enormously from the successful integration of AI. To engage them, one should involve them right from the inception, asking questions about their most menial, tedious, time-consuming, or high-stakes tasks.

By identifying areas in their workflows that involve mundane tasks, individuals become more inclined to accept AI intervention as they see directly how it benefits them. For instance, a sales team might welcome a solution that automates lead generation and categorization, allowing them to focus on closing sales rather than scouting for prospects.

The buy-in from internal stakeholders also depends on providing clear information and appropriate training. This helps stakeholders understand that AI is a tool set to augment, not replace human capabilities. Continuous examples of how decision-making can be enhanced and human capabilities can be augment will lead to higher buy-in and an overall smoother integration process.

Turning to **external stakeholders**, engaging them with AI is about leveraging the technology to improve their interactions with your organization. Customers, for example, stand to benefit from AI-driven customer service tools. Smart chatbots can provide 24/7 support, handling simple queries, while freeing up human personnel to tackle more complex issues.

Customers receive faster, more accurate responses, and feel more satisfied with the service, leading to increased engagement.

Similarly, shareholders would be interested in how the use of such tool transforms profitability, operational efficiency, and mitigates risks. Real-world examples, such as cost savings from AI-led automation or revenue gains from AI-enabled personalized marketing, can help engage and convince shareholders of the implicit benefits and at the very least will give you a few exciting talking points for your next shareholder meeting.

Remember, every stakeholder has different expectations and concerns about AI. Engaging them effectively requires a clear understanding of their needs, t ransparent communication, and tangible demonstrations of AI's potential benefits and returns. With the right engagement strategy, an organization can foster a robust culture of AI acceptance that benefits everyone involved.

MAXIMIZING ROI BY IMPLEMENTING GEN-AI

The essence of maximizing ROI by implementing Gen-AI collates comprehending the value of this investment and leveraging its full potential for a long-term business enhancement outlook.

Understanding what counts as a return in the AI context is important in maximizing the ROI. Here, it's essential to realize that returns from Gen-AI stretch beyond traditional profit margins to include comprehensive business enrichment. AI systems can automate mundane tasks, reduce costs, and improve process efficiencies, all contributing to quantitative returns. Simultaneously, they enhance the ability to innovate, streamline decision-making processes, and unlock new potentials, which constitute qualitative returns.

For instance, investing in Gen-AI for product design development could initially yield **efficiency savings** as designs that used to take weeks now get ready within minutes. That's your **'Automation Savings'**. Yet, as the system becomes better integrated into workflows and learns from progressive iterations, **progressional** efficiency gains' additional benefits spring up unexpectedly. Projects once considered unfeasible due to extensive lead times suddenly become significant income generators; these are your **'Revealed Opportunities'**.

Such unfolding of opportunities stimulates you to ponder over "What hidden layers of ROI might our system reveal as we continue down the road of implementation and integration?" You're presented with a growth landscape that encourages you not just to focus on the current efficiencies gained but also to anticipate future enhancements to your operations.

The pursuit of maximizing ROI involves more than just aiming for immediate payback; it necessitates directing resources towards staff training, system integration, debugging — foundational elements critical for reaping long-term benefits. This initial phase is merely about paving the way for future productivity enhancements rather than realizing immediate returns.

Pairing this expansionist perspective with traditional business mathematics provides us with a holistic formula that accommodates some unique gains from Gen-AI:

ROI = (Initial Savings + Progressional Efficiency Gains + Revealed Opportunities - Initial Costs) / Initial Costs

This formula aids strategic leaders in comprehending potential gains better while focusing on their long-term strategy towards increased productivity and substantial business value.

Maximizing AI ROI isn't exclusively about strict monitoring or exerting controls; it's more about understanding its comprehensive impact and exploiting its prospective capabilities with an eye on sustainable growth and advancement. Only then can you navigate profitably through the vast ocean of its capabilities. This marks the true success of implementing AI — optimizing business modalities today while paving paths for novel opportunities tomorrow.

HARNESSING GEN-AI IN **BUSINESS OPERATIONS**

Exercise 3:

Document your organization's core processes. Identify tasks that are repetitive or mundane and consider how AI could streamline these tasks.

Exercise 4:

Map out a plan to engage and educate all stakeholders about your AI operations. This could include town-hall style meetings, newsletters, or seminars.

*Detailed exercise guides can be found in the appendix

3
COGNITIVE OFFLOADING AND GEN-AI

In this chapter we delve deeper into the intriguing potential AI holds to relieve intellectual burden, allowing your team to focus on more critical and creative tasks. Specifically designed for CEOs and decision-makers, this chapter aims to equip you with knowledge and insight on how AI can be a cognitive force multiplier for your organization. We will explore how offloading repetitive and mundane tasks to AI can significantly boost productivity and job satisfaction, creating a happier, more enthused workforce. Moreover, we'll touch on how Gen-AI can outperform human capacity in specific areas, thereby accelerating your business processes and amplifying your return on investment. By the end of this chapter, you'll understand the power AI has to transform the way we work and have practical insights on deploying AI to nurture a workforce that is agile, innovative and engaged. We encourage you to use the knowledge gained from this chapter to revolutionize your organization and propel your team to new heights.

> *KPMG uses generative AI chatbots to handle common employee HR queries on payroll, time- off requests etc. This cognitive offloading enables HR to focus on more strategic tasks.*

Source: *https://advisory.kpmg.us/perspectives/2021/automating-the-future-workplace.html*

PRESERVING HUMAN COGNITION

Preserving human cognition is now more crucial than ever in the rapidly evolving world of business. This critical resource influences everything from decision-making to problem-solving and is directly linked to a company's success. Hence, it's crucial to find ways of preserving and enhancing this asset. Here's where Gen-AI comes into play.

As previously discussed, it can meaningfully assist in preserving human cognition by handling repetitive and menial tasks. Machine cognition can step in to take over regular tasks like data analysis, report generation, appointment scheduling, and even customer interactions. Consider the day-to-day routine of a customer service representative. They could spend countless hours fielding basic inquiries that could be easily handled by AI algorithms. By automating these tasks, employees are free to engage their cognitive abilities on complex problem-solving and strategizing. The saved human cognition can then be utilized for creative tasks, strategic planning, and innovation.

Processing large amounts of data often leads to mistakes and oversights due to human error. **Taking on large amounts of unstructured data and turning it into structured outputs that are defined by the user, is one of the main skills of Gen-AI today.** For instance, analyzing market trends from complex and diverse data sources can be laborious and could lead to oversight due to cognitive exhaustion. AI algorithms can quickly sift through this information and provide actionable insights, reducing the cognitive load on humans and decreasing the chances of human errors.

When it comes to augmentation, it offers fast, data-based insights that save the time required for data gathering and analysis, giving employees more time to apply their cognitive resources to interpret the results and make informed decisions. In an R&D department, for instance, AI-based tools can scan existing patents or research papers, present a synopsis, and even suggest new areas of innovation based on trends, all at a pace far beyond human capability. The experts can then use their cognition to brainstorm and develop new ideas, instead of just gathering and organizing information.

The smart use of Gen-AI can act as a protector and amplifier of human cognition, freeing minds from tedium and enabling them to focus on the creative, strategic elements of a company's growth. Preserving human cognitive resources in this way leads to an engaged and motivated workforce which ultimately drives the business's success. By creating an environment where AI and human cognition work in harmony, businesses can unlock significant potential.

ENHANCING PRODUCTIVITY AND SATISFACTION

Productivity is the lifeblood of any organization, and the introduction of Gen-AI has taken it to another level by automating mundane tasks and ushering in increased efficiency. Consider the example of a business analyst, inundated with piles of data reporting and analysis tasks. Traditionally, these require intensive manual effort, consuming a significant chunk of their workday. Gen-AI can be an excellent ally for such roles—rather than spending countless hours combing through data and generating reports, the analyst can delegate this task to their AI counterpart.

The AI system, equipped to handle vast amounts of data, combs through the information, identifies patterns, and presents an analysis in a fraction of the time, allowing the analyst to focus on interpreting the data and making strategic recommendations. This shift elevates their role from a data processor to a strategic influencer, hugely benefiting the organization. By focusing on high-value tasks, employees can use their skills to the fullest extent, increasing the overall productivity quotient of the team.

Let's consider the psychological impacts of repetitive tasks and how AI could help. Mundane work often leads to disengagement and burnout, hurting job satisfaction. But imagine an AI-powered work environment. Routine tasks get automated, freeing people to focus on creative thinking and innovation that adds value.

Take a movie production coordinator who spent most time organizing schedules and logistics, leaving little room for creative input. With AI systems automating scheduling and coordination, the coordinator now focuses on higher-level creative tasks like providing input on storyboards and character development.

This transformation not only improves coordinator satisfaction by reducing drudgery, but also enhances creativity and productivity. More human energy gets channeled into imaginative, strategic work rather than repetitive logistics.

The same holds true across roles. Automating mundane tasks allows people to devote time to complex and rewarding responsibilities, eliminating tedium and improving satisfaction. AI systems can reshape workflows to maximize human creativity and potential.

> *The generative AI market is projected to grow from $4.3 billion in 2022 to $62.5 billion by 2032 at a CAGR of 31.7%*

Source: *https://www.emergenresearch.com/industry-report/generative-ai-market*

WHY OUTPERFORMING HUMANS IS A GOOD THING

Implementing the right workflows can lead to immense ROI gains where machines outpace human limitations. But this requires thoughtful adoption.

For repetitive high-volume tasks like invoice processing or customer service queries, AI excels without fatigue. Imagine a global retailer that automated invoice handling with AI, cutting costs by 50% while operating 24/7.

Another example could be an investment firm boosting trading profits 15% by having AI quickly analyze market data and pinpoint profitable opportunities.

By taking over dull, tedious tasks and amplifying cognitive ones, staff focus more on high-value strategic work. A software company could find that engineers spent 25% more time on innovation after AI took over performance testing and bug fixing.

However, relying too heavily on these systems has its own risks. Over time, human skills can atrophy. Model biases can creep in without oversight. Change management and training are vital to prepare staff for more collaborative roles.

The key is identifying the right mix of AI automation and human talent. Set metrics to continually track ROI gains from AI implementation. But also monitor risks like over- dependence. With responsible adoption, AI can deliver significant ROI gains in the right workflows by augmenting and exceeding human capability. But the human element remains indispensable.

A COGNITIVE FORCE MULTIPLIER

In the extent of modern business operations, Gen-AI stands as a veritable cognitive force multiplier, supercharging human capabilities whilst providing relief from strenuous cognitive labor. Imagine working on a complicated report which depends on the analysis of an exhaustive set of data. Traditionally, processing this data and extracting meaningful insights would require several hours or even days of diligent manual labor. However, with the help of Gen-AI, this task can be seamlessly accomplished in a far shorter timespan, and with no compromise on quality of outputs as long as it's used correctly.

This is where the power of cognitive offloading comes to the fore. By allowing AI to take over data crunching tasks and generate insightful summaries, individuals are then able to leverage their cognitive abilities to interpret these insights towards constructive decision making. AI does the heavy lifting of reviewing and processing the data, while humans can focus on applying their judgement, empathy, and experience towards making decisions that can drive business growth.

Consider a marketing team working on a creative advertising campaign. By using Gen-AI tools that can brainstorm ideas, extend existing content, and draft new versions, they can generate an array of creative options far quicker than humanly possible. Thus, rather than exhausting their cognitive power in creating numerous iterations, they can direct their energies and creativity towards evaluating and fine-tuning the best options for the campaign.

For instance, while the AI may supply a gamut of creative options for the advertising campaign, the final decision on what will resonate best with the target audience garners significant reliance on human experience, intuition, and judgement. The key lies in harmonizing the computational prowess of AI with human wisdom to yield the best results.

Acting as a cognitive force multiplier, Gen-AI can give businesses a significant upper-hand in a competitive marketplace by relieving cognitive load, hastening operations, and enhancing the scope for human creativity and strategic thinking. However, preserving human cognition remains pivotal, dictated by the principle that while humans can leverage AI, there's no substitute for human judgement, empathy, and innate creativity.

COGNITIVE OFFLOADING AND GEN-AI

Exercise 5:

Conduct a time study of your team's activities over a week. Identify tasks that could be delegated to AI, freeing up your team's mental bandwidth for more strategic tasks.

Exercise 6:

Ask your employees for their perspective on tasks they would feel comfortable offloading to AI, as well as those tasks they would prefer to keep.

*Detailed exercise guides can be found in the appendix

4 GEN-AI AND EFFECTIVE
LEADERSHIP

This chapter focuses on the seamless marriage of Gen-AI and effective leadership. We explore the profound ways in which these tools and platforms can be leveraged to build stronger, more prosperous business relationships and promote a culture of respect, trust, and dignity, even in this tech-driven era. Understand the critical role of leaders in promoting the ethical use of data and protecting privacy.

As a leader, evolutionary self-improvement is a constant pursuit. Learn how Gen-AI aids in self-reflection, honing your decision-making skills, and catalyzing your leadership capabilities. This chapter provides actionable insights into how it can help you lead from the front and become a beacon of technological advance within your organization.

By the end you will not only have gained some insight on the integration of AI in your leadership style but also heightened your personal growth curve. Moreover, you will be equipped to foster an organizational culture that respects and ethically utilizes AI, rallying your team around shared success and synchronized growth. Remember, in the world of AI, the journey of growth and adaptation is not a lonely road but a shared highway towards collective success.

> *AI could contribute over $13 trillion to the global economy by 2030*

Source: https://www.pwc.com/gx/en/issues/data-and-analytics/publications/artificial-intelligence-study.html

BUILDING STRONGER RELATIONSHIPS WITH AI TOOLS

In today's fast-paced, tech-driven world, knowing how to cultivate strong relationships using AI tools is a crucial leadership quality. Many might ask how machine learning or algorithms can contribute to improved relationships. The key lies in using AI's capabilities to foster communication, boost employee empowerment, enable top-notch decision-making, and facilitate personalized interactions.

Think of a business scenario dealing with an extensive team scattered across different geographical locations. Given the current technology-led work environments, teams heavily rely on online communication tools. This is where AI can help. Advanced AI tools not only streamline communication but also detect subtle nuances like sentiment in texts, helping leaders to understand their team's mood and issues better. This means you can respond to your team's concerns more effectively, thus building trust and credibility.

Moreover, AI tools can be utilized to democratize decision-making. For example, rather than always depending on the hierarchy to make decisions, these AI tools can produce data-driven insights that empower all levels of the workforce to make informed decisions. This not only promotes transparency but also saves valuable decision-making time. Consequently, it enhances job satisfaction and boosts productivity, forming the bedrock of positive relationships in the team.

Illustrating this idea, let's take the case of a multinational company that successfully employed AI tools to revamp its decision-making processes. By analyzing internal data, the AI model generated valuable insights on performance, customer preferences, product lines, etc. These insights were made available across the organization, allowing employees at all levels to make informed decisions. This not only improved efficiency but also positively impacted relationships as the workforce felt valued and empowered.

Personalized interactions also play an essential role in building strong relationships. With AI's help, you can analyze patterns and preferences, enabling you to tailor your communication to suit individual needs. You can use these insights to recognize and appreciate your team's efforts in a way that resonates with them. This not only improves your rapport with the team but also enhances overall team morale.

In essence, the ability to leverage Gen-AI tools is not just a technical skill — it is also an art of leadership which leads to stronger professional relationships. By harnessing AI's potential in enhancing communication, democratizing decision-making, and personalizing interactions, you can foster a work environment that values transparency, inclusion, empowerment, and high morale. And these ingredients lay the foundation for robust, thriving business relationships.

Consider the case of Sarah, a project manager overseeing a large, geographically dispersed project. Initially, she spent significant time managing emails, detracting from strategic tasks. Recognizing this inefficiency, Sarah deployed an AI email management tool leveraging natural language processing (NLP) and machine learning.

The tool categorized emails by urgency, content, and sentiment, drafted initial responses for simple queries based on Sarah's past data, and flagged emails with negative sentiment. The implementation of the AI tool significantly reduced Sarah's email management time, enabling her to focus on critical project tasks. Improved response time fostered trust within her team, and the sentiment analysis helped anticipate issues, allowing for proactive problem- solving. Automating routine responses enabled Sarah to craft personalized messages for complex queries, strengthening her relationship with the team.

Consequently, the AI tool boosted Sarah's productivity while fostering stronger, more effective relationships with her team, illustrating how AI can significantly enhance leadership and workplace productivity.

SELF-REFLECTION AND LEADERSHIP

An effective leader knows the importance of self-reflection. It not only provides insights into how individuals think and act but can lay the foundation for personal growth and exceptional decision-making. But in the hustle-bustle of managing complex operations, self-reflection often takes a back seat. This is where advanced AI tools like Chat GPT, Claude other conversational AIs can play a crucial role.

For instance, AI-powered reflective journaling tools can help you track your thoughts, feelings, and motivations behind decisions. This process helps highlight patterns and trends that you might not consciously consider. By consistently revisiting these entries, you are not only better informed about your decision-making processes but also about the inherent biases or flawed reasoning you may need to work on. As a result, this enhanced self-awareness can make you even more effective in your role.

The use of this technology goes beyond simply processing information; it can offer new angles to tackle problems.

As a fitting example, let's consider the scenario of a record label manager in the music industry. Confronted with a pivotal decision on the artistic direction for an upcoming album, she turned to Gen-AI for possible creative paths. Gen-AI was able to analyze patterns in current music trends, the artist's past work, and audience preferences, generating various musical direction scenarios. Some of these scenarios validated her instincts, while others presented fresh, innovative angles she hadn't thought of before. This process prompted her to question her initial assumptions, identified gaps in her strategy, and uncovered perspectives that she had previously overlooked.

While AI provides perspective, insights, alternatives, and recommendations, it's necessary to remember the importance of human judgment and oversight.

As you can see, it can hold massive potential for employee training and development. Traditional training materials sometimes fail to engage or motivate employees. By crafting interactive experiences and engagement-enhancing features, you can create more effective training materials. Imagine a scenario where AI suggests skill development courses to employees based on current business trends or market conditions. This not only ensures relevance but also encourages employee involvement in their own development.

These tools can act as companions to your leadership journey. By providing a mirror to your thought processes and offering novel perspectives, you can become a leader fitted for the future. It demands active involvement and openness to challenging your preconceived notions. As an AI- augmented leader, you become more aware, more informed, and consequently, exponentially more effective.

> *Dell Technologies trains its sales team on AI ethics and responsible use principles before deploying an AI- based customer chatbot. This maintains trust and transparency.*

Source: *https://www.forbes.com/sites/markminevich/2022/06/29/responsible-and-ethical-ai- considerations-and-impact/?sh=3c0f61db6c8d*

MAINTAINING TRUST, DIGNITY, AND RESPECT

The integration of Gen-AI into our professional landscape involves profound changes at all levels. As exciting as it may be, this transition also presents new challenges, particularly around trust, dignity, and respect. In this AI age, leaders need to maintain the delicate balance between leveraging AI's powers and preserving individual rights and dignity.

Trust forms the cornerstone of successful, progressive organizations, and integrating AI doesn't change that principle. However, it does add a new dimension to it. Often, there is trepidation around the misuse of AI or a lack of understanding about its function - both of which can erode trust between leaders and their teams. The key is to confront these issues head-on. Leaders need to explain how AI will be used, who will have access to it, and how it will benefit the organization. The aim should always be to generate an open dialogue and restore faith in the process.

For instance, a retail company planning to implement AI in their supply chain management system clearly communicated their AI integration plan to all stakeholders, detailing out how collected data would not be misused, rather used solely to improve operational efficiency. By doing so, they not only diminished fears about privacy breaches but also gained the much-needed trust of their team.

Dignity, another essential facet of effective leadership, becomes more critical when AI comes into the fray. It's vital to use AI in a way that augments human dignity. That means AI should never supersede respect for individuals' rights, privacy, and emotions. Whether used in HR evaluations or customer interactions, the application of AI must be guided by principles that respect our shared humanity.

Respect plays a pivotal role during the induction of AI into the workforce. A balanced approach towards Gen-AI involves weighing its benefits against potential ramifications on individuals. Decisions should be ethical, and align with a deep respect for human rights and well-being. Sometimes, this might mean mitigating job displacement fears due to AI or addressing psychological effects of interacting with machines.

In essence, the AI era calls for responsible and ethical leadership. It's about earning and maintaining trust, preserving individual dignity, and respecting human rights. By adhering to these guiding principles, you can navigate the AI- wave successfully, ensuring it aligns with organizational values and fosters a culture of fairness and empathy. The future lies in our abilities to harness AI's powers responsibly and ethically for shared growth.

PRIORITIZING PRIVACY AND ETHICAL USE OF DATA

Incorporating Gen-AI into a corporate setting requires a keen understanding and commitment to data privacy and ethics. The crux lies in how personal and sensitive data is handled while focusing on respecting human rights. This is particularly relevant now as, more than ever before, a significant amount of data is being harnessed to train and fine-tune AI models.

At the heart of privacy preservation is ensuring the secure handling of customer, employee, or stakeholder data. This involves not just utilizing encryption or advanced cybersecurity measures but building processes that inherently respect confidentiality. For instance, a health insurance company safeguarded privacy when incorporating AI by anonymizing all patient data before using it to train their prediction models. By stripping personal identifiers, they ensured that no sensitive data could be traced back to individuals.

Alongside privacy, ethical use of data stands as the other pillar of responsible AI integration. This involves several dimensions, from how data is sourced and used for training AI models to the real-world consequences of these models. Obtaining data ethically means transparency with individuals about their data usage and ensuring consent. Once this is done, the next checkpoint is to see if the model itself is fair and devoid of biases. Discriminatory practices can be consciously or unconsciously embedded in AI systems, resulting in biased outcomes. Therefore, it becomes essential to instill measures that prevent such outcomes.

A leading technological company sets a great example of practicing data ethics. It opened channels for employees to voice concerns about ethical implications in their AI models, enabling a system where potential biases could be reported and addressed. This move demonstrated their commitment to avoid discriminatory outcomes of their AI systems.

Being a leader in the AI era requires you to create a culture of responsible data practices. Adhering to privacy regulations, fostering transparency, and accountability should be your top priority. It is about anchoring the implementation and use of AI technologies around trust, dignity, and respect. Remember, going forward, privacy and ethical use of data will not just be regulatory requirements but also critical value propositions that distinguish companies. By prioritizing these aspects, you stay ahead in the AI space while nourishing an ethically sound AI culture within your organization.

SELF-IMPROVEMENT FOR LEADERS

In the journey of leadership, one's growth and development never stop. The exponential advancements in AI offer unique opportunities for leaders to further this growth. Gen-AI, in particular, provides several avenues for self-improvement, acting as a cognitive tool that can elevate a leader's abilities in reflection, decision-making, and strategic planning.

Consider the potential of AI as an avenue for reflection. Leaders can utilize AI tools to track their thoughts, behaviors, and decisions. These insights can reveal subconscious patterns, biases, or tendencies that might go unnoticed otherwise. For instance, an AI tool could reveal a leader's inclination to favor certain kinds of solutions over others, making them aware of possible blind spots in their decision- making.

Moving a step further, Gen-AI can also bolster leaders' decision-making process. Today, leaders can employ AI models that generate multiple scenarios or viewpoints based on large-scale data points. This breadth of perspectives supports the leader in making an informed decision. An example of this is how many automobile companies use Gen- AI to analyze and predict market trends and customer preferences, thereby enabling leaders to make smart decisions about new car features or marketing campaigns.

Additionally, AI tools can enhance the reasoning and strategic planning of leaders. With AI's ability to analyze complex data and predict future scenarios, strategizing becomes significantly more efficient. For an illustration, an e- commerce leader used an AI model to anticipate future product demands based on historical data and trending indicators. The insights gained aided that leader in mapping out a more effective inventory and supply chain strategy.

Collectively, Gen-AI makes leaders more reflective, more informed, and more strategic; all of which are fundamental to self-improvement and effective leadership. It's not just about using AI to automate tasks or processes; it's about how AI can help leaders augment their own cognitive abilities and become better at what they do. Embracing Gen-AI is to welcome a partnership where man and machine work together towards cognitive enrichment and leadership advancement. This is the cutting edge of self-improvement in our AI-enabled world.

Let's look at the weekly routine of a fictional CEO, John, who employs AI tools to refine his leadership skills. He uses an AI journaling tool to recognize patterns in his decision- making and highlight areas for growth. An AI decision support system provides him with diverse solutions for critical decisions, challenging his viewpoints. Finally, he reviews an AI-generated report that evaluates his strategic choices and helps optimize his approach, fostering continuous self- improvement.

THE CEO'S GUIDE TO **GENERATIVE AI**

GEN-AI AND EFFECTIVE
LEADERSHIP

Exercise 7:

Reflect on your own leadership style and consider how you can use AI to improve. This could be as simple as using AI to manage your schedule more effectively or as complex as analyzing data to inform strategic decisions.

Exercise 8:

Develop a policy statement outlining your organization's commitment to ethical data use and privacy. Review it with your team and solicit feedback.

*Detailed exercise guides can be found in the appendix

5 NAVIGATING THE IMPACT OF GEN-AI

Let's delve into the profound implications that this technological advancement can have on the landscape of your business operations. As a leader, you need to be equipped to harness these changes and turn them into valuable opportunities. By understanding the cost-efficiency and enhanced productivity delivered by AI, you can better capitalize on these tools to cultivate a competitive edge.

You will see how AI can contribute to novel areas such as creativity and art within your enterprise, forging new avenues of innovation. We'll also navigate how strategic planning can reach new heights with AI, bolstering your business's foresight and decision-making ability even in complex scenarios.

We address the darker side of automation as well as potential job loss and the accompanying ethical considerations. You'll gain practical insights into how to balance automation and human roles, maintaining a harmonious and respectful workplace while staying ahead in the AI era.

Finally, you'll appreciate the dynamic opportunities and threats that AI brings forth. You will know how to prepare for and manage these risks, steering your organization confidently into the future. You will emerge from this chapter with a comprehensive understanding and a realistic perspective of both the challenges and opportunities that Gen-AI can create for your business. In essence, this chapter serves as your navigation guide on the complex road to AI integration, leading to fruitful business transformations.

QUANTIFYING AI'S COST SAVINGS

Implementing Gen-AI offers immense potential for cost savings across business functions. But quantifying the benefits requires a long-term outlook.

Cost reductions often come from automating repetitive tasks like customer service, reporting, and data entry. Chatbots alone have saved companies thousands in call center staffing needs.

Process optimization is another savings avenue. AI can identify and eliminate workflow inefficiencies, bringing lean operations. Supply chain AI could reroute shipments to avoid delays, lowering logistics costs.

However, harness savings opportunities responsibly. AI should align with ethics, not just economics. Avoid over- automation that could dehumanize the workplace.

View savings as means, not the objective. Reinvest resources saved into upskilling staff and innovation. With the right approach, AI-driven efficiency enables new capabilities.

Calculate savings across years, not quarters. Expect an initial investment in technology, training and integration. But savings typically repay this and compound with AI maturity.

Set ROI metrics like reduced processing times, error rates and operational costs. But also track productivity gains, revenue opportunities and customer satisfaction.

Savings require change management. Prepare staff for evolving roles and new skills needed alongside AI. A difficult transition can erase economic gains.

Take the example of a successful online learning platform, EdFutura. EdFutura harnessed AI to automate customer service, which significantly reduced its operational costs. Their AI chatbot handled 75% of customer queries, saving thousands of dollars annually by reducing their customer service staff requirements.

Moreover, by using AI to identify bottlenecks in course content delivery, EdFutura could optimize its processes and minimize delay-induced costs. Additionally, EdFutura used AI to personalize learning paths for students, leading to an increase in course completion rates and customer satisfaction.

Initially, integrating AI required investment, but over a three-year period, EdFutura not only recouped this expenditure but also saw a 20% decrease in operational costs and a 35% increase in productivity. In essence, their prudent AI adoption strategy paid off.

UNLOCKING VALUE

A Fictional ROI Case Study of Nova Skin TL;DR

- Nova Skin integrates Gen-AI into its operations for a competitive advantage.
- Automation of package design saves $45,000 annually. Swift adjustments to designs based on customer preferences and market trends lead to increased sales of $120,000 per year.
- Marketing promotions around limited-edition packaging generate an additional $80,000 in annual revenue.
- Initial costs for Gen-AI implementation are $25,000.
- The calculated ROI for Nova Skin's Gen-AI integration is 960%.
- Gen-AI empowers Nova Skin in product design, market responsiveness, and profitability.

In the competitive world of skincare, companies are constantly on the lookout for ways to gain an edge. Let's look at a fictional case study of a skincare company called Nova Skin that implements Gen-AI, transforming their business processes and ROI.

Nova Skin manufactures skincare products including creams, serums, cleansers and more. They are preparing to launch a new anti-aging face cream. Traditionally, designing the packaging and marketing for a new product took weeks across multiple teams. But now, Nova Skin is harnessing the power of Gen-AI.

They deploy an AI system that can generate hundreds of viable packaging designs by learning from past successful designs and customer preferences data. This automated design process reduces the timeline from weeks to just hours.

Previously, Nova Skin's packaging design costs including staff and software licenses was $50,000 annually. Their new AI system cost $20,000 to implement and $5,000 for yearly operating costs. This results in an initial direct cost savings of $25,000 from packaging design automation (($50,000 - $5,000) = $45,000).

As the AI model continues learning, Nova Skin can make rapid adjustments to packaging based on updated customer preferences and industry trends. This agility leads to increased sales of $120,000 per year by avoiding losses from outdated designs.

Additionally, the quick design iterations enabled by the AI system opened new marketing possibilities. Nova Skin creates special limited-edition packaging for holidays, generating $80,000 more in annual revenue.

Given the $25,000 implementation costs, Nova Skin's ROI from their Gen-AI integration is calculated as:

ROI = ($45,000 + $120,000 + $80,000 - $25,000) / $25,000 = 960%

By tapping into Gen-AI, Nova Skin unlocked tremendous value through design automation, market agility, and innovative promotions. Their example showcases the transformative potential of AI in enhancing productivity, creativity, and ultimately, profitability.

CREATIVITY AND ART IN THE AI DOMAIN

At the intersection of business, creativity, and art, Gen-AI emerges as a transformative force. Its implications reach beyond conventional norms, suggesting that AI isn't strictly about automating routine processes or crunching colossal amounts of data. By providing fresh perspectives and innovative ideas, Gen-AI can stimulate a fertile ground for human creativity and artistic endeavors.

Imagine a scenario in a marketing firm where a new advertising campaign is being planned. Typically, human teams brainstorm, iterate, and refine ideas over weeks. Integrating Gen-AI into this process can supercharge creative ideation. The AI, trained on vast troves of past advertising data, can suggest novel concepts and taglines that the human team might not have considered, sparking unique angles and approaches. It's like having an extra team member with a completely different creative lens to look through.

The use of automated and streamlined parts of the creative process can have huge benefits. For example, in graphic design, AI can generate initial design templates based on specified parameters. This eliminates hours spent by designers on basic concepts, offering them more time and mental freedom to focus on nuanced design elements and introduce their unique artistic flair.

Just remember that the AI's role is the one of an assistant, the human touch in creativity remains irreplaceable. This is where judgment, intuition, and cultural context come into play, giving true depth to an idea or piece of art. Gen-AI may propose a catchy slogan for a brand, but contextual interpretation, emotional resonance, and final decision-making still fall into the human purview.

To maximize the potential of Gen-AI in enhancing creativity and art within a business, the key is to find the right synergy. Utilize AI for ideation, inspiration and mundane tasks, while reserving the inviolable human facets—judgment, empathy, and inherent creativity. This ensures that innovative and artistic outcomes remain compelling and culturally sensitive, while the process becomes more efficient and expansive through AI. In an ever-evolving business landscape, this blend of human creativity and artificial intelligence could shape a new epoch of artistry and ingenuity.

Samsung's AI researchers are exploring using generative AI to create personalized digital avatars for video calls and virtual environments.

This could enable highly customized metaverse experiences in the future.

Source: *https://research.samsung.com/blog/samsung-research-america-ai-center-explores-new-frontiers-in-generative-ai*

STRATEGIC ANALYSIS AND REASONING

Strategic analysis and reasoning are cornerstones in business. Deciding which markets to penetrate, how to outshine competitors, where to allocate resources, and countless other complex considerations. Gen-AI is stepping up as a valuable ally to businesses in these intricate workings.

Take the common scenario of market strategy formulation. Intense competition, socio-economic fluctuations, and rapid market dynamics make it challenging to devise an efficient and adaptable strategy. Enter Gen-AI. This intelligent system, trained on a vast trove of historical market data and figures, can aid strategists like never before. With precise and real- time market trend forecasts, AI not only reduces the guesswork but also offers clear competitive analysis to help managers identify potential opportunities and threats.

By intelligently scrutinizing internal operational data, Gen- AI can highlight areas where performance can be optimized. For instance, an AI system can analyze data points from various departments, identify underperforming areas or cost overruns, and suggest remedial action. This provides an unbiased and holistic view of the organization and aids in swift and accurate performance-driven decisions.

Gen-AI is also making great strides in scenario analysis. Given a set of constraints and goals, AI can generate multiple viable approaches or strategies. For example, in the case of product launch scheduling, AI can evaluate factors such as historical sales data, competitors' activity, market conditions, and logistical considerations to suggest the best timing schedule.

Complex strategic decisions often involve ethical considerations, cultural nuances, and sometimes gut intuition, areas where AI is still developing its proficiency. Therefore, the crux of effective AI utilization rests in integrating its increasingly sophisticated capabilities with the unique qualitative insights that human decision-makers offer.

With Gen-AI in your strategic arsenal, the enhanced depth of analysis, forward-looking insights, and varied perspectives can help break through complex problem spaces, enhancing the caliber, efficiency, and agility of strategic decision-making in a volatile business landscape.

HARMONIZING AI AND HUMAN DEVELOPMENT

The swift evolution of AI presents a unique opportunity for accelerated learning and superior decision-making across various industries. As the tools for digitization continue to progress, strategic integration becomes paramount to fully capitalize on their potential.

Successfully incorporating these advancements within an organization hinges on the strategic assignment of tasks. Automation can significantly bolster efficiency across multiple domains, from data processing to customer service. However, the essence of integrating these technologies isn't about the complete replacement of human roles; instead, it focuses on fostering a symbiosis between human intellect and mechanized processes.

Achieving balance in this digital transformation involves pinpointing areas ripe for automation — where efficiency can significantly increase without undermining the inherent value of human roles or dampening morale. Striking this balance is pivotal for seamless integration and overall operational harmony.

Moreover, as technological tools become more embedded in daily operations, the roles and responsibilities of employees inevitably undergo changes. In this evolving landscape, upskilling becomes the cornerstone for organizational success. Upskilling involves more than just understanding new technologies; it also involves nurturing cognitive abilities that enhance decision-making and problem-solving skills.

An organization dedicated to thriving in this modern era prioritizes training and skill development, cultivating an environment where employees evolve in tandem with the technological advancements, continually adapting, learning, and growing.

ADDRESSING JOB LOSS AND OTHER CHALLENGES

Embracing intelligence tools like Gen-AI doesn't inherently precipitate job losses. Rather, it provokes a transformation, causing a role evolution where routine tasks yield to more strategic, creative, and interpersonal ones. This shift isn't a threat but an opportunity to redefine work by reallocating human talent to tasks demanding ingenuity and empathy.

The story of job displacement due to automation isn't a tale of eradication, but one of metamorphosis. Consider the image of a caterpillar morphing into a butterfly. The creature doesn't vanish; it changes form, acquiring new capabilities. In a similar vein, roles in an organization don't disappear. They evolve, becoming more nuanced and demanding higher- order skills.

Managing this shift warrants attention. It requires proactive planning, akin to navigating a ship through changing waters. The guiding compass should be a strategy that ensures the well-being of employees while aligning with the larger vision of the company. A well-planned transition not only leverages the power of intelligence tools, but also reassures employees, positioning them to thrive in a transformed work environment.

Getting everyone on board the transformation journey requires transparency and dialogue. Clear communication around the integration of tools like Gen-AI and the changes it may bring can help alleviate fears and build trust among employees. Their involvement in this process is essential to success, making them active participants in the change, not just passive observers.

NAVIGATING NEW CAPABILITIES, OPPORTUNITIES, AND THREATS

As you chart your path in today's competitive business landscape, the transformative power of Gen-AI offers a veritable trove of capabilities and opportunities. Whether you aim to supercharge productivity, enhance the quality of work, or multiply cognitive force, these advancements can serve as invaluable allies. Take the manufacturing sector as an example, where the integration of Gen-AI has improved product consistency, accelerated defect detection, and ultimately, reduced costs and bolstered brand reputation.

But as you reap these rewards, remember that such power doesn't come without its share of challenges. The integration of these technologies into established workflows necessitates meticulous planning to prevent disruption and preserve employee satisfaction. Moreover, navigating this new terrain responsibly is crucial. The potential for privacy infringements and over-dependence on algorithmic decisions are real concerns that require appropriate safeguards.

Whether you're keen to ride this wave or not, remember: your competition likely is. In such a scenario, it's no longer just about wielding the potential of Gen-AI, but also about taming its risks. Striking the right balance is the linchpin to success. This entails appreciating the magnitude of Gen-AI's potential, preparing for inevitable hurdles, and ensuring the ethical use of technology throughout your business.

In essence, tapping into the potential of Gen-AI is akin to Pandora's box—it's filled with remarkable possibilities but also hosts its share of challenges. Being aware of these facets and staying equipped to handle them ensures you're well-positioned to harness the transformative potential of AI without compromising ethical standards.

THE CEO'S GUIDE TO **GENERATIVE AI**

NAVIGATING THE IMPACT OF GEN-AI

Exercise 9:

Identify potential risks and opportunities related to AI in your organization. Create contingency plans to mitigate the risks and capitalize on the opportunities.

Exercise 10:

Discuss potential job loss due to automation with your team and gather their input on retraining or upskilling opportunities. Develop a plan that respects current employees while taking advantage of AI benefits.

*Detailed exercise guides can be found in the appendix

CLOSING THOUGHTS

The world of Gen-AI holds astounding potential, yet can seem daunting in its complexity. As you reach the end of this guide, take comfort in knowing you don't need to master every technical detail or implementation yourself.

The key is cultivating your curiosity about how AI can transform your business. Whether you directly oversee an AI integration or bring on specialized talent, let this book ignite your vision for an AI-powered future.

Remember, integrating AI is a journey of gradual immersion, not an overnight overhaul. Move forward, one step at a time. Experiment with AI capabilities that solve your most pressing problems first. Build on small wins to expand strategically.

If it all seems too complex, consider hiring or appointing a Chief AI Officer. Task them with spearheading your AI initiatives. Leverage their expertise to navigate AI adoption at a pace suitable for your organization.

Stay abreast of developments in the AI space. But don't get lost in the noise. Be judicious in adopting new capabilities. Let practical needs, not fleeting hype, drive your technology decisions.

The AI landscape will keep evolving rapidly. Accept this state of fluidity. Stay nimble and open-minded as you iterate your AI strategy. Expect setbacks along the way. Persist through the ambiguities.

Remember your core values. Implement AI-driven changes ethically and responsibly. Progress does not necessitate compromise on principles. With vision and wisdom, harness AI's potential for shared benefit.

I hope this guide illuminated AI's transformative power for your business. May your AI journey lead to unprecedented possibilities. Let me conclude with an encouragements - the future belongs to the curious. Go forth and explore.

I enjoy engaging in thought-provoking conversations about AI and the future of business. If you would like to connect after reading this guide, you can find me on **Twitter at @kamilbanc** and on **LinkedIn - Kamil Banc**. You can also always reach out directly via **kbanc.com** Feel free to reach out with your thoughts, questions, or ideas - I'd be delighted to hear from you. Continuing the dialogue on the fascinating developments in AI is what inspires me, and I hope my insights have illuminated your path forward. Let's keep the conversation going!

Let me know if you would like me to modify or expand this paragraph in any way. I'm happy to update it with your exact social media handles and links. Making it easy for readers to connect with you allows for engaging future discussions to continue beyond the book.

APPENDIX

Exercise Guide — 78

Exercise 1: Identifying Areas for AI Improvement — 79

Exercise 2: Brainstorming Future AI Innovations — 80

Exercise 3: Documenting and Streamlining Core Processes — 81

Exercise 4: Stakeholder Engagement and Education — 82

Exercise 5: Conducting a Time Study for Cognitive Offloading — 83

Exercise 6: Employee Perspective on Cognitive Offloading — 84

Exercise 7: Reflecting on Your Leadership Style and Identifying AI Applications — 85

Exercise 8: Ethical Decision-Making for AI Implementation — 86

Exercise 9: AI for Creativity and Innovation — 87

Exercise 10: Preparing for the Future Impact of AI — 88

FAQ — 89

Frequently asked questions on Generative AI for Executives and business Leaders — 89

Glossary — 97

EXERCISE GUIDE

EXERCISE 1:
IDENTIFYING AREAS FOR AI IMPROVEMENT

Objective: Identify areas of your business that would benefit from automation or enhanced decision-making capabilities.

Instructions:

Step 1: **Identify the Key Business Functions**: Begin by identifying and listing all the key functions in your business. This could range from HR, marketing, and sales, to operations, finance, and product development.

Step 2: **Analyze Each Function**: For each function, analyze and list down all the core activities. These should include both repetitive, mundane tasks as well as strategic decision-making processes.

Step 3: **Identify Pain Points**: For each activity, ask yourself: 'Is this process efficient? Does it add significant value to the organization? Can it be improved?'

Step 4: **Create a Wish List**: After identifying potential pain points, create a wish list of areas where you'd like to see improvements. Also, consider how AI could potentially address these areas.

Step 5: **Prioritize Your List**: Based on the impact on the overall business, time spent on tasks, and feasibility of implementing AI solutions, prioritize the list.

Step 6: **Engage a Team or Expert**: Depending on the complexity of the processes identified, consider engaging a team or AI expert to explore and implement potential solutions.

EXERCISE 2:
BRAINSTORMING FUTURE AI INNOVATIONS

Objective: Engage your team in a brainstorming session to imagine what future AI innovations could look like in your organization.

Instructions:

Step 1: **Schedule a Brainstorming Session:** Schedule a brainstorming session with key team members across different levels and functions in your organization. A diverse team will provide a wide range of perspectives.

Step 2: **Set the Agenda:** Set the agenda for the session, clearly defining its purpose. Make sure all participants understand what is expected of them.

Step 3: **Generate Ideas:** Encourage participants to express their thoughts on how AI can be incorporated in the future. Ensure a safe space for sharing ideas and feedback without judgment.

Step 4: **Discuss Fears and Concerns:** Open a dialogue about fears, hopes, and expectations for AI. This can include potential job losses, privacy concerns, or fears about the unknown.

Step 5: **Prioritize Ideas:** Have the team vote on the ideas they think are most valuable, feasible, and impactful for the business. Prioritize these for further exploration.

Step 6: **Action Plan:** Assign responsibility to individuals or teams to explore the prioritized ideas further, assess feasibility, and develop implementation plans.

EXERCISE 3:
DOCUMENTING AND STREAMLINING CORE PROCESSES

Objective: Identify tasks in your organization's core processes that are repetitive or mundane and consider how AI could streamline these tasks.

Instructions:

Step 1: **List Core Processes:** Identify and list all the key processes that drive your business. For instance, in a sales organization, this could include lead generation, client outreach, deal negotiation, and closing.

Step 2: **Detail Each Process:** Break down each core process into the specific tasks that make it up. You might find it helpful to create a flowchart or process map.

Step 3: **Identify Repetitive Tasks:** For each task, ask: 'Is this task repetitive or mundane? Does it consume a significant amount of employee time? Can it be automated?'

Step 4: **Assess AI Suitability:** For the tasks identified in step 3, evaluate the potential for AI to take over. Consider factors such as the complexity of the task, the quality of data available, and the potential for improvement in efficiency or effectiveness.

Step 5: **Document Opportunities for AI:** For each task where AI could potentially be used, document the current process, the potential AI solution, and the expected benefits.

Step 6: **Implement AI Solutions:** With the help of your technology team or an external partner, explore AI solutions that fit your needs. Begin implementing these on a trial basis, monitor the results, and adjust as necessary.

EXERCISE 4:
STAKEHOLDER ENGAGEMENT AND EDUCATION

Objective: Map out a plan to engage and educate all stakeholders about your AI operations.

Instructions:

Step 1: **Identify Stakeholders:** Begin by identifying all internal and external stakeholders who have an interest in or are affected by your organization's AI initiatives. This could include employees, board members, customers, investors, and partners.

Step 2: **Determine Information Needs:** Understand what each group of stakeholders needs to know about your AI operations. For employees, this might include how their jobs will change. Customers might want to know how AI will improve the products or services they receive.

Step 3: **Develop Communication Plan:** Create a comprehensive communication plan to keep stakeholders informed. This should specify what information will be shared, who will share it, when and how it will be communicated, and who the audience for each message is.

Step 4: **Execute the Plan:** Put your communication plan into action. Use a variety of communication methods, such as meetings, newsletters, or seminars, to ensure your message reaches all stakeholders.

Step 5: **Feedback Mechanism:** Establish a mechanism for stakeholders to ask questions, provide feedback, and express any concerns. This could be a dedicated email address, a suggestion box, or regular Q&A sessions.

Step 6: **Review and Adjust:** Regularly review and adjust your communication plan based on feedback from stakeholders and changes in your AI operations.

EXERCISE 5:
CONDUCTING A TIME STUDY FOR COGNITIVE OFFLOADING

Objective: Identify tasks within your team's activities that could be delegated to AI, allowing for more focus on strategic tasks.

Instructions:

Step 1: **Announce the Time Study:** Notify your team about the upcoming time study. Explain the purpose and how the information will be used to potentially improve efficiency.

Step 2: **Conduct the Time Study:** Have each team member record how they spend their time over the course of a week. This should include all tasks, no matter how small. The goal is to get an accurate picture of how time is currently being used.

Step 3: **Analyze the Results:** Collect the data and analyze the results. Identify tasks that consume a significant amount of time, especially those that are repetitive or don't require a high level of skill or decision-making ability.

Step 4: **Identify Opportunities for AI:** For tasks identified in step 3, assess whether AI could take over or assist in these tasks, thereby freeing up your team's mental bandwidth for more strategic tasks.

Step 5: **Develop a Plan:** Develop a plan to implement AI solutions for the tasks identified. This could include researching and selecting AI tools, training team members on how to use the tools, and monitoring progress and results.

EXERCISE 6:
OFFLOADING EMPLOYEE PERSPECTIVE ON COGNITIVE

Objective: Gather input from your employees on tasks they would feel comfortable offloading to AI, and those they would prefer to keep.

Instructions:

Step 1: **Schedule a Meeting or Survey:** Set up a meeting or anonymous survey where employees can share their perspectives. Explain the purpose of the meeting or survey to your team.

Step 2: **Ask for Input:** Ask employees for their perspective on tasks they would feel comfortable offloading to AI, and those they would prefer to keep. This may be influenced by their interest in the tasks, their perceived importance of the tasks, and their comfort level with AI.

Step 3: **Discuss Concerns:** Allow employees to voice any concerns they may have about AI taking over certain tasks. Address these concerns openly and honestly.

Step 4: **Document Feedback:** Document the feedback received from the employees and analyze it to identify trends, concerns, and opportunities.

Step 5: **Use Feedback in AI Planning:** Use this feedback to inform your AI implementation plan. Where possible, address the concerns raised by employees and involve them in the process.

EXERCISE 7:
REFLECTING ON YOUR LEADERSHIP STYLE AND IDENTIFYING AI APPLICATIONS

Objective: Identify how AI can assist in your leadership tasks and enhance your decision-making abilities.

Instructions:

Step 1: **Leadership Tasks Identification:** List the key tasks that you undertake as a leader. These could be strategic planning, employee management, decision-making, etc.

Step 2: **Evaluate Your Strengths and Weaknesses:** For each task, critically assess your strengths and weaknesses. Consider where you excel and where you could improve.

Step 3: **Identify AI Assistance Opportunities:** Determine where AI could assist you. For instance, AI could help you analyze data more effectively, freeing you up to make strategic decisions.

Step 4: **Create an AI Implementation Plan:** Once you've identified where AI can assist you, create a plan for implementing the necessary tools. This might involve researching various AI tools, obtaining any necessary training, and setting a timeline for implementation.

Step 5: **Monitor Progress:** Regularly review and assess your progress. Make necessary adjustments and celebrate the improvements AI brings to your leadership tasks.

EXERCISE 8:
ETHICAL DECISION-MAKING FOR AI IMPLEMENTATION

Objective: Understand and implement an ethical decision-making process when integrating AI into your organization.

Instructions:

Step 1: **Define Ethical Guidelines:** Create a set of ethical guidelines that reflect your organization's values and principles. These guidelines will serve as a compass for your AI-related decisions.

Step 2: **Identify Potential Ethical Challenges:** Brainstorm potential ethical challenges related to AI use in your organization. These might include concerns about job losses due to automation, privacy issues, data security, bias in AI algorithms, and transparency.

Step 3: **Evaluate AI Solutions:** Evaluate potential AI solutions against your ethical guidelines. Consider how each solution aligns with your guidelines, and identify any potential issues.

Step 4: **Stakeholder Discussion:** Involve all key stakeholders in the decision-making process. Discuss potential solutions, along with their benefits and potential ethical challenges. Make sure everyone understands the implications and has a chance to voice their opinions.

Step 5: **Create an Action Plan:** Based on the evaluation and discussion, create an action plan to implement AI solutions that align with your ethical guidelines. This plan should include steps to mitigate any potential ethical issues.

Step 6: **Monitor and Revise:** Once your plan is in place, regularly monitor its implementation and its effects. Be open to revising the plan as necessary to address any unforeseen ethical issues or to incorporate new AI advances.

EXERCISE 9:
AI FOR CREATIVITY AND INNOVATION

Objective: Identify areas in your business where AI can stimulate creativity and foster innovation.

Instructions:

Step 1: **List Key Business Areas:** Create a list of key business areas within your organization that have potential for creative enhancement or innovation. This might include product design, marketing campaigns, customer service, etc.

Step 2: **Explore AI Creativity Tools:** Research AI tools that can foster creativity and innovation. These might include tools for generating new design ideas, content creation, trend prediction, etc.

Step 3: **Identify Potential AI Applications:** Match the AI tools from Step 2 with the key business areas from Step 1. Identify how each tool could be used to foster creativity or innovation within these areas.

Step 4: **Create an Implementation Plan:** For each AI application identified in Step 3, create an implementation plan. This might include acquiring the necessary tools, training staff, and setting a timeline for implementation and review.

Step 5: **Review and Adjust:** Once the tools are in place, regularly review their impact on creativity and innovation within your organization. Be open to adjusting your approach based on the results.

EXERCISE 10:
PREPARING FOR THE FUTURE IMPACT OF AI

Objective: Understand and prepare for the long-term impacts and risks of AI implementation in your organization.

Instructions:

Step 1: **List Potential AI Impacts:** List the potential long-term impacts that AI could have on your organization. Consider both positive impacts (e.g., improved efficiency, cost savings, etc.) and negative impacts (e.g., job losses, privacy concerns, etc.).

Step 2: **Assess Risk Levels:** For each potential impact, assess the risk level. Consider both the likelihood of the impact occurring and the severity of the consequences if it does occur.

Step 3: **Develop Mitigation Strategies:** For each high-risk impact, develop a mitigation strategy. This should include steps to prevent the impact from occurring, if possible, and to manage the consequences if it does occur.

Step 4: **Implement Mitigation Strategies:** Put your mitigation strategies into action. This might include changes to your AI implementation plan, staff training, development of contingency plans, etc.

Step 5: **Monitor and Review:** Regularly monitor the impacts of AI on your organization and review your risk assessment and mitigation strategies. Be prepared to make changes as necessary to manage emerging risks.

FAQ

Frequently Asked Questions On Generative Ai For Executives And Business Leaders

1. **HOW CAN GENERATIVE AI IMPROVE PRODUCTIVITY AND CUSTOMER ENGAGEMENT?**

   Generative AI offers a transformative approach to enhancing productivity and engaging customers. By analyzing extensive volumes of both structured and unstructured data, generative AI can provide immediate and accurate insights. These insights can form the backbone of informed decision-making, strategy formulation, and process optimization, acting as a powerful catalyst for driving business efficiency and growth[2]. Furthermore, generative AI plays a pivotal role in predicting industry trends, arming businesses with the foresight needed to stay competitive in a rapidly evolving market landscape. On the customer engagement front, generative AI serves as an invaluable tool for processing user feedback, developing intricate customer personas, exploring unique value propositions, and crafting customized marketing campaigns. The use of generative AI in these areas can result in highly personalized and engaging customer experiences, ultimately driving customer satisfaction and loyalty[2].

2. **WHAT ARE THE PRIMARY CONCERNS REGARDING GENERATIVE AI ADOPTION?**

   The journey towards generative AI adoption comes with its set of concerns, the most prominent being issues related to quality and control, as well as safety and security risks. Quality and control are critical factors that govern the success of generative AI implementations, ensuring the consistency, accuracy, and reliability of the AI's output to align with business objectives and customer expectations[1]. Safety and security risks revolve around the protection of the AI system and the data it handles from potential threats, emphasizing the importance of robust cybersecurity measures[1]. Beyond these primary concerns, businesses face challenges related to ethical issues, data privacy, worker displacement, misinformation, plagiarism, copyright infringements, and harmful content generation. These challenges underline the need for comprehensive risk management strategies and robust monitoring and control mechanisms in the realm of generative AI[6].

3. **HOW CAN GENERATIVE AI IMPACT ORGANIZATIONAL ROLES?**

The adoption of generative AI brings significant changes to the organizational landscape. As businesses increasingly integrate generative AI into their operations, it's estimated that 90% of business leaders foresee considerable impacts on specific job roles within their organizations[5]. This change is expected to spur the emergence of new roles that cater specifically to the needs of AI, such as AI auditors and AI ethicists. These roles will be instrumental in ensuring responsible and ethical AI operations, from monitoring AI systems for bias and fairness to ensuring adherence to regulations and ethical standards. While this transition may necessitate reskilling and upskilling initiatives, it ultimately leads to a workforce that's well-equipped to harness the full potential of generative AI[5].

4. **WHAT ARE THE POTENTIAL BENEFITS AND RISKS OF GENERATIVE AI?**

Generative **AI offers a** myriad **of benefits that can revolutionize** how businesses operate. Among **these** benefits, improved productivity stands out prominently. By automating repetitive tasks and providing insights for decision making, generative AI can significantly enhance work efficiency. Beyond productivity, generative AI can spur work transformation, reshaping jobs, and creating new roles tailored to an AI-driven environment.

Furthermore, generative AI can be a catalyst for innovation, fueling new ideas and approaches to problem-solving. However, generative AI is not without risks. If not managed correctly, it can negatively impact organizational trust, leading to reputational damage. Moreover, clarity in the business case for generative AI is essential to justify investment and to guide its implementation. Implementing generative AI can pose challenges, especially given the technical complexity and the need for expertise in AI[10].

5. HOW CAN BUSINESSES ENSURE ETHICAL USE OF GENERATIVE AI?

Ensuring the ethical use of generative AI is a paramount concern for business leaders. To foster ethical use, businesses must establish robust AI Ethics & Governance mechanisms. This includes creating a well-defined AI strategy that outlines the goals, applications, and boundaries of AI use within the organization. Good governance is also crucial. It involves setting up structures and processes to oversee AI operations, ensuring they align with ethical standards and regulatory requirements. Moreover, a commitment to responsible AI is essential. This involves promoting fairness, transparency, privacy, and security in AI operations. By fostering a culture of ethical AI use, businesses can leverage generative AI's benefits while mitigating potential risks[12].

6. WHAT ARE THE TECHNICAL CHALLENGES OF GENERATIVE AI?

Generative AI models are often highly complex, containing billions or even trillions of parameters. This complexity can pose significant challenges for businesses, particularly those without a strong background in AI. These models require considerable computational resources to train and deploy, which can be impractical with standard hardware. Furthermore, managing such models can require advanced expertise in AI and machine learning, which may not be readily available in many organizations. These technical challenges underline the importance of carefully considering the resources and expertise needed when adopting generative AI[11].

7. **HOW CAN GENERATIVE AI FIT INTO A COMPANY'S DATA/AI STRATEGY?**

Incorporating generative AI into a company's data/AI strategy is a strategic decision that requires careful consideration of the organization's AI maturity and readiness to adopt advanced technology. Generative AI should align with the broader data and AI roadmap, serving as a tool that enhances the organization's existing AI capabilities rather than a standalone solution. With its ability to generate new data and ideas, generative AI offers potential opportunities for enhancing customer experiences through personalization and developing new business models. For instance, generative AI can be used to create personalized content or recommendations, improving customer engagement and satisfaction. Furthermore, it can spur innovation by generating novel ideas and solutions, potentially leading to the development of new products, services, or business models[9].

8. **WHAT EDUCATION PROGRAMS CAN BE IMPLEMENTED TO ENSURE EMPLOYEES CAN WORK EFFECTIVELY WITH GENERATIVE AI?**

To ensure employees can work effectively with generative AI, companies should invest in comprehensive training and development programs. These programs should aim to equip employees with a thorough understanding of generative AI, including its capabilities, applications, limitations, and ethical considerations. For instance, employees should be trained on how to use generative AI tools, interpret their outputs, and apply them in their work. Moreover, they should learn about the ethical implications of using generative AI, such as the potential for bias or misuse, and how to mitigate these risks. Such training can be delivered through various formats, such as workshops, online courses, or hands-on projects, and should be tailored to the needs and skills of different employee groups. Through continuous learning and development, employees can be empowered to harness the full potential of generative AI in their work[9].

9. HOW CAN GENERATIVE AI BE USED TO DRIVE ENTERPRISE VALUE AND ACHIEVE BUSINESS OBJECTIVES?

Generative AI can serve as a powerful tool for driving enterprise value and achieving business objectives. By aligning generative AI with the overall business strategy, companies can leverage its capabilities to drive innovation, improve customer experiences, optimize processes, and create new business models. For instance, generative AI can be used to generate novel ideas for products or services, improving a company's competitive position. It can also enhance customer experiences by providing personalized content or recommendations. Moreover, by automating routine tasks and providing insights for decision making, generative AI can optimize business processes, improving efficiency and productivity. Finally, generative AI can enable the development of new business models, such as those based on personalized services or data-driven insights[14].

10. WHAT ARE THE KEY CONSIDERATIONS FOR MANAGING THE RISKS OF GENERATIVE AI?

Managing the risks of generative AI is critical to ensuring its responsible and effective use. Recognizing the need to manage risks is the first step. These risks can include security threats, biased outcomes, and ethical concerns. Security involves protecting the AI system and the data it handles from cyber threats. Bias relates to ensuring the AI operates fairly and does not discriminate against certain groups. Ethical concerns involve ensuring the AI's use aligns with moral principles and societal norms. Implementing robust governance is a key strategy for managing these risks. This involves setting up structures and processes to oversee AI operations, ensuring they align with ethical standards and regulatory requirements. Monitoring mechanisms are also crucial for detecting and addressing issues promptly. These mechanisms can include audits, reviews, and AI systems that monitor the operation of other AI systems. Additionally, control mechanisms are needed to manage the AI's operations and prevent misuse. These mechanisms can include rules, guidelines, and technical controls that limit what the AI can do[16].

CITATIONS:

[1] https://venturebeat.com/ai/business-leaders-fret-about-generative-ai-despite- growing-adoption/

[2] https:// www.forbes.com/sites/forbesbusinessdevelopmentcouncil/ 2023/06/28/5-potential-impacts-of-generative-ai-within-the-enterprise-sector/? sh=e0fd49660f13

[3] https://venturebeat.com/ai/business-leaders-investing-generative-ai-automation-reinvent-physical-operations/

[4] https://www.seriousinsights.net/ten-questions-every-business-will-be-asking- about-generative-ai-next-year/

[5] https://www.capgemini.com/news/press-releases/74-of-executives-believe-the- benefits-of-generative-ai-will-outweigh-the-associated-concerns/

[6] https://www.techtarget.com/searchenterpriseai/tip/Generative-AI-ethics-8-biggest-concerns

[7] https://hbr.org/2023/04/generative-ai-will-change-your-business-heres-how-to- adapt

[8] https://www.linkedin.com/learning/generative-ai-for-business-leaders

[9] https://www.linkedin.com/pulse/boardroom-briefing-10-essential-questions-directors-ai-baluwala-ph-d

[10] https://decrypt.co/144011/generative-ai-enormous-impact-business-execs-admit-not-right-away/

[11] https://www.techtarget.com/searchenterpriseai/tip/Generative-AI-challenges- that-businesses-should-consider

[12] https://www.ibm.com/blog/exploring-generative-ai-to-maximize-experiences- decision-making-and-business-value/

[13] https://careerconnections.smeal.psu.edu/classes/generative-ai-for-business-leaders/

[14] https://www.linkedin.com/pulse/unlocking-power-generative-ai-20-essential-questions-chakkarapani

[15] https://technologymagazine.com/articles/capgemini-report-generative-ai-benefits-to-offset-concerns

[16] https://hbr.org/2023/06/managing-the-risks-of-generative-ai

GLOSSARY

Advisory AI   An AI system that provides guidance or advice, like suggestions or recommendations, in decision-making processes.

Algorithm   A set of rules or instructions that a computer follows to solve a problem or complete a task.

Analytics   The practice of analyzing data to draw insights and make informed decisions.

Anomaly Detection   The identification of rare, unusual, or unexpected patterns in data, a common application in AI security.

API (Application Programming Interface)   A set of software rules and specifications that allows different software applications to communicate and interact with each other.

Artificial Intelligence (AI)	The simulation of human intelligence (AI) processes by machines, especially computer systems including learning, reasoning, and problem-solving.
AI Hallucination	When an AI system generates content that is completely fabricated and inaccurate, like a false memory. Often due to insufficient training data.
Automation	The use of machines to perform tasks that would otherwise be done by humans
Automated Reasoning	Techniques used within AI that allow automatic manipulation and interpretation of high-level abstractions or concepts.
Autonomous Systems	Systems capable of performing tasks with little to no human intervention, often powered by AI.
Augmented Reality (AR)	The integration of digital information with the user's environment in real time.

GLOSSARY

Bias Correction — Techniques used to mitigate biases in an AI system, especially those arising from training data.

Big Data — Huge volumes of structured and unstructured data that can be analyzed for insights leading to better decisions and strategic moves.

ChatGPT — A conversational AI system created by Anthropic to interact in natural language and answer questions on a wide range of topics.

Chief AI Officer (CAIO) — An executive role focused on developing an organization's AI strategy, accelerating adoption, and ensuring responsible implementation.

Cloud Computing — The delivery of computing services over the internet, providing accessibility and scalability benefits for AI systems.

Cognitive Computing — A type of computing that aims to mimic the human brain's cognitive functions such as learning, problem-solving, and decision-making.

Cognitive Offloading	The concept of delegating intellectual workloads to machines, resulting in cognitive respite for the human counterparts.
Collaborative Filtering	A popular method used in recommender systems where recommendations are made based on user similarity.
Computer Vision	The ability of machines to interpret and understand visual information.
Conversational AI	Technology that enables machines to engage in human-like dialogues, made possible with natural language processing (NLP) abilities.
Cybersecurity	The protection of computer systems and networks from theft, damage, or unauthorized access.
Data Aggregation	Combining different data sources into a single, comprehensive dataset used in AI training or analysis.

GLOSSARY

Data Annotation — The process of providing information to datasets, often to train machine learning models.

Data Cleaning — The process of identifying and correcting inconsistencies, inaccuracies, and errors in datasets used for AI model training.

Data Mining — The process of discovering patterns and knowledge from large volumes of data.

Data Visualization — The presentation of data in a pictorial or graphical format which provides valuable insights into complex datasets.

Deepfake — AI-generated synthetic media in which a person's likeness is replaced with somebody else's.

Deep Learning — A type of machine learning that uses neural networks to learn from data.

Edge Computing — A distributed computing concept that brings computation closer to the source of data generation, improving response times and saving bandwidth.

Ensemble Learning — A machine learning concept where multiple models are trained to solve the same problem and combined to get better results.

Feature Engineering — The process of creating new features or modifying existing features in the dataset to improve model performance.

Feature Extraction — The process of identifying and selecting important variables from raw data for use in model building.

Federated Learning — A technology that allows machine learning on decentralized devices or servers holding local data samples without sharing them.

GLOSSARY

Generative AI — Algorithms capable of creating new, original data that closely resembles the patterns and relationships in their training data. Unlike predictive AI, generative AI models can produce new content, designs, sounds, etc. rather than just categorizing data. This offers businesses creative applications, from generating product designs to creating personalized customer content at scale.

Generative Pre-trained Transformer (GPT) — an artificial intelligence model developed by OpenAI that uses deep learning to generate human-like text. It is trained on vast datasets to predict probable next words based on the context. Versions like GPT-3 demonstrate increasing conversational ability.

Heuristic — A rule-of-thumb or simplified approach used to speed up the process of finding satisfactory solutions by an AI system.

Hyperparameters — These are adjustable parameters within an AI model that determine how quickly it learns during training.

Image Recognition	A subfield within computer vision where machines are trained to interpret and categorize what they see in images or visual data feeds.
Information Retrieval	This involves extracting the required information from unstructured documents or sets of documents stored electronically for use in AI systems.
Intent Recognition	Used in conversational AI, it involves the machine understanding the goal or purpose behind a user's input.
Internet of Things (IoT)	The network of physical devices, vehicles, home appliances, and other items embedded with electronics, software, sensors, and connectivity which enables these objects to connect and exchange data.
Knowledge Graphs	A knowledge base that uses a graph-based structure to represent, integrate, and share complex structured and unstructured information.

GLOSSARY

Knowledge Representation — It refers to organizing all the information so that AI can understand and use it efficiently.

Labelled Data — In supervised learning models this term refers to data where each piece has been tagged with one or more labels highlighting specific attributes.

Latent Variables — Variables that are not directly observed but inferred through a mathematical model from other observed variables.

Machine Learning (ML) — An AI application that provides systems the ability to automatically learn and improve from experience without explicit programming.

Model Training — Process of teaching an AI model with a given dataset and algorithms until it can predict outcomes accurately.

Midjourney — An AI system that generates unique images and artwork from text prompt descriptions provided by the user.

Natural Language Generation (NLG)	Sub-field of AI focusing on generating natural language narratives coherently from structured data inputs.
Natural Language Processing (NLP)	The ability of machines to understand and interpret human language
Neural Network	A type of algorithm modeled after the structure of the human brain that can learn from data.
Outlier Detection	Identifying instances that deviate significantly from other observations in a dataset—a critical aspect of data cleaning.
Predictive Analytics	Utilizing statistical algorithms and machine learning techniques to identify future outcomes based on historical data.
Prescriptive Analytics	Part of business analytics that uses predictive models to suggest various course of actions to decision-makers.

Prompt	Instructions given to an AI system to provide context and guide the desired response. Well-crafted prompts allow users to get optimized results from AI systems like chatbots or generative models.
Prompt Engineering	The crafting of effective prompts to provide AI systems with optimal context and parameters to get the desired output.
Quantum Computing	Advanced computing technology leveraging quantum mechanics' principles to process extensive amounts of data and perform complex calculations rapidly.
Reinforcement Learning (RL)	Area within ML involving agents learning how to behave by performing actions that lead to rewards.
Robotic Automation	Utilization of robots powered by AI and ML algorithms to automate repetitive manual tasks in businesses enhancing productivity.
Robotics Process Automation (RPA)	Use of software robots or 'bots' powered by AI algorithms to automate repetitive tasks.

Semantic Analysis — Part of NLP involving the understanding of meaning and context within text data sources used in conversational AI systems.

Sentiment Analysis — Application of NLP techniques to identify, extract, understand the sentiments expressed in text data.

Smart Contracts — Self-executing contracts with terms of agreement directly written into lines of code. They provide secure transactions without third parties on blockchain technology.

Supervised Learning — Machine learning technique where models learn from labeled training data to make predictions or decisions without being explicitly programmed to do so.

Swarm Intelligence — Collective behavior of decentralized, self-organized systems that find application in optimizing problems, predicting social behaviors, or robotics among others.

GLOSSARY

Time-series Analysis — Techniques used to analyze time-series data to extract meaningful statistics and identify patterns over time.

Transfer Learning — ML method where a pre-trained model is fine-tuned for a similar but different task than its original purpose.

Unsupervised Learning — Type of ML where model learns without labeled training data by finding patterns in input.

Validation Set — Subset of training dataset used to evaluate a model during training phase for hyperparameter tuning and ensuring robustness against overfitting.

Virtual Reality (VR) — A computer-generated simulation of a three- dimensional image or environment that can be interacted with in a seemingly real or physical way by a person using special electronic equipment.

Voice Recognition — Technology that recognizes and interprets human speech enabling voice-controlled applications.

THE CEO'S GUIDE TO **GENERATIVE AI**

Web Scraping — Practice of extracting large amounts of data from websites using intelligent automation software. Often used for gathering datasets for training ML models.

Workflow Automation — Use of rule-based logic to automate manual tasks making processes more efficient.

Yield Optimization — In marketing scenarios, the use of algorithms to determine best strategies for customer engagement and revenue growth.

Zero-shot Learning — A type of learning where the AI model can fruitfully handle situations it has not seen before during training.

Printed in Great Britain
by Amazon